# 200 Prayers

# Written for

# the Mórrígan

200 Prayers Written for the Mórrígan


by C. A. S.

Cover art: Cynth AB Salas

Printed in the United States of America

ISBN 979-8497121933

*An Mór Ríoghain,*

*Giver of battle poetry and prophecy,*

*Inciter of the battle,*

*Bringer of change,*

*Present on the battlefield,*

*Sacred sovereignty,*

*fistfuls of blood,*

*Prophecies, sorcery, shape-shifting,*

*Satirist, wielder of magic,*

*Pleasure in mustered hosts,*

*Incitement of the warrior, strategist,*

*Guardian of the land,*

*Bestowing of rulership,*

*Demanding of sovereignty,*

*Washer at the ford,*

*Giving prophecy of doom,*

*Death to kings with broken geasa,*

*Restorer of right rulership,*

*Sovereignty eternal.*

**Table of Contents** **Pages**

# Introduction

Thank you for your interest in this book. This collection of prayers was written as an expression of personal devotion to the Mórrígan and as an offering to fulfill a commitment made with her. I'm sharing it for publication with the sincere hope that it provides inspiration or content for other devotees of the Mórrígan (or potential devotees) in the writing of their own prayers. Please freely use or alter the prayers found here for personal use in any way, public or private, that honors An Mórrígan or any of Na Mórrígna. Even if these prayers are just a reflection of who the Mórrígan is to me, I hope they may be beneficial to support the practice of others in some way.

Please take note of any literal or implied promises written in a prayer before using it. Many of these prayers have a commitments written in them that are personal to me (I also knowingly use words like always, forever, and at least one prayer uses the phrase "this lifetime and the next"). Please alter any wording to what is appropriate for you and your relationship with the Mórrígan. If you are new to working with the Mórrígan, or unsure of who the Mórrígan is, I personally recommend doing research and building a relationship before making any commitments. If you are new to the Mórrígan, I would also like to suggest exploring the information provided by Lora O'Brien at the Irish Pagan School (IPS) as a starting point as well as the playlist on the Mórrígan by Lora O'Brien on YouTube. I have truly found that playlist to be an invaluable collection of reliable content on the Great Queen. The current links for some recommended content can be found at: https://loraobrien.ie/morrigan/ and https://loraobrien.ie/morrigan-irish-mythology/

I would like to share how this book came about. This project began after an assignment during the "Meeting the Mórrígan 6 Month Intensive" program with Lora O'Brien at the Irish Pagan School (they run the Intensive Program annually and information can be found at https://irishpaganschool.com). There was an assignment in that included writing a prayer. I had naively held that idea that I had written lots of prayers when actually it was less than ten. After a few conversations with the Great Queen and receiving the Mórrígan's generous aid with something I needed, I had agreed to write a book of prayers (with a requirement of 200 prayers including the original handful I had already written, and it had to be done by Samhain). As a result, this devotional project has consumed my life for the past five months (I was still required to do my offerings and other commitments to her, with some allowances thankfully, as well as maintain my mundane job and family needs). I HAD to complete this project. In the end, I had to prove to her that I could complete this task. Today it is October 30, 2021. It is completed on time, edited, being uploaded, and I am grateful.

Let me segue into recommendations. Before certain sections I share recommendations that are based on my personal experiences. I do not claim to be an expert on the Mórrígan and I do not claim to speak for her. These recommendations that I share are based on my personal beliefs. Please be aware that the content of this book is based on my personal gnosis (UPG) and should be taken as such. Relationships with deity can be potentially different for everyone, so of course please disregard any recommendations that don't resonate with you. I have appreciated writing out the recommendations, as it helped me clarify my own beliefs and thought processes. That being said, this work is not intended to teach or alter anyone's existing personal understanding. These prayers were written for the Mórrígan and are based on my personal relationship with the Great Queen. This book contains my own UPG, and as these prayers will reflect, my relationship with her includes veneration.

That all being said, most of these prayers include petition with praise elements as well. Some of the prayers are written in the context of asking for significant aid or even an intervention, such as the sections on change or protection. I recommend adding the details of the situation to the petition and perhaps also any specific results or boundaries that are needed. If making a promise in exchange for aid, I advise being specific with what you are offering in exchange, including time-frames and asking for necessary resources. I have made agreements to do work for her in exchange for her aid. Her help has been provided her way, however she sees fit for resolving the situation, and the results have often been unexpected ones. I can confidently say that the end result was always more beneficial than what I had anticipated, but sometimes there were adjustments in my own life that had to occur as well.

While this book was written in agreement with her, not many prayers were written with her close guidance, but I believe that a few were, including the prayer for doing a formal contract with the Mórrígan. However, as strange as this may sound, I cannot encourage taking that action. I included it because I was directed to do so by the Mórrígan. The Mórrígan is not a Goddess to make agreements with lightly. She is deserving and demanding of respect and there can be consequences for breaking agreements with her. As with all such books, I make no promises and take no responsibility for results. No prayers are a substitute for medical attention, treatment, or any other support you may be in need of. I do not provide any steps for ritual in this book; it is simply a collection of prayers.

Also, be aware that there are no scholarly sections in this book explaining who the Mórrígan is, her lore, or her history. The prayers are separated into categories according to the petition or theme. Some portions of the sections may read as one long prayer and others will read as different versions of the same prayer. Finally, you'll see the names An Mórrígan, An Mór Ríoghain, the Great Queen, Mórrígu, and the Mórrígan used interchangeably (these all mean "The Great Queen" for those that may not know). Na Mórrígna is the plural, and is used to refer to her as a collective, such as when speaking of the Mórrígan, Badb, Macha, Anu, Fea, and/or Bé Neit.

Full disclosure, I am not Irish and I do not wish to be appropriative of Ireland or the Irish people with this work. While I cannot say it is a requirement to work with the Mórrígan, it is my deep belief that it is respectful to give back to the Irish people and Ireland while working with her. The Mórrígan is a Goddess of Ireland. If you decide to work with the Mórrígan, please consider how you can hold space for Ireland and its people.

There is one Irish phrase included in most of the prayers and I apologize upfront if I have made any errors. I've tried to be careful. "Go raibh maith agat" is Irish for "thank you" and to my understanding it would be pronounced differently depending on which part of Ireland you are in. I recommend Teanglann.ie as a good resource for Irish pronunciation. I pronounce it similar to "Gur-rah mah-hAgut" (I tried to be careful, but please look it up and hear it for yourself. I described it the way I hear it and it may not be accurate). Go raibh maith agat is used when speaking to one person. Go raibh maith agaibh is used when speaking to more than one person and would be appropriate if you're altering a prayer to be said to Na Mórrígna. Some prayers reference specific details from information found in the Irish lore. I did add a reference list at the end of the book to go over some of those details, but it is a brief list. What I truly want to emphasize is that there are a few recommendations for books, YouTube videos, and classes from experienced scholarly content providers, writers, and teachers who all provide a wealth of information and guidance. Those sources are where to go if you are new to the Mórrígan, in my opinion, and are all worthy of exploring.

For anyone that has made it through to the end of the introduction, thank you. It is my great joy to share these prayers and I am grateful to anyone who comes across them. As for myself, I'm a faithful devotee with a lifelong commitment and a great love for the Mórrígan.


My extreme gratitude to Mara for her generous help with editing and feedback.

## General Daily Prayers

1.

Honor to you, An Mórrígan.

Great Queen, hear my prayer.

Battle crow that incites the battle for sovereignty and watches it on the battlefield,

Giver of triumph, bringer of great change, I honor you.

Goddess to whom I have promised my effort and work,

May I begin this day with the resolve to complete it.

May I complete, to our satisfaction, the work before me.

May I keep my focus and have clarity in my goals.

May I act with honor and with rightness.

As I go about my many tasks, may safety stay upon me, Great Queen.

May I receive your guidance at all times needed in my life.

When you look at me, Goddess, may you find me doing the work.

May my promises always be kept to you.

May I honor you by doing the work you give me, An Mórrígan.

Goddess of sovereignty, I honor you.

Go raibh maith agat.

2.

An Mórrígan, I call to you with respect. Hear my prayer, Goddess.

Washer at the ford, giver of prophecy,

See the usefulness I may have for you.

May I aid you in your strategies for change and your great work,

In whatever ways I am able.

As we work together and I learn, An Mórrígan,

May my understanding and intuition be accurately aligned.

May I be careful about my projections

And may my actions be aligned with honor.

May I do the work needed to live my life with rightness.

May I honor the sovereignty of myself,

And honor the sovereignty of others with respect.

May I respect the spaces I enter,

And the boundaries of others.

May I stay aware of my own needs, and maintain my self care

As I give hospitality to the needs of others.

May my mind be quiet as I do my work.

May I listen. May I hear.

Thank you for your time and your guidance, Great Queen.

Honor to you, An Mórrígan.

Go raibh maith agat.

3.

An Mórrígan, hear my prayer.

Goddess of prophecy and sovereignty,

Goddess of battle, bringer of change,

Guide me to do the work I need to do,

And may that work honor us both.

May I fight the battles that I must fight,

And may I only fight the battles worthy of me.

May I have accountability for myself,

For the way I treat myself and my environment.

May I seek out the ways I can encourage growth

And beneficial changes within myself.

May I invest in my own growth with persistence

And be unafraid of what the future will bring.

Thank you, Great Queen, for your time.

Go raibh maith agat. I honor you, An Mórrígan.

4.

An Mórrígan, Goddess of battle whose pleasure is in mustered hosts,

Defender of sacred sovereignty, I call out to you.

I bring you offerings from what I have, Goddess.

I offer you my willingness to do the work you bring to me,

In truth and loyalty, and with constancy.

I will honor you daily and do the work that is required

To honor my authentic self, to honor both life and death,

And to journey through the depths of my own darkness

As needed for my growth and healing.

May I remember that I am worthy of self-sovereignty, self-care, and self-love.

I thank you for your time and your presence in my life.

I call to you with respect, An Mórrígan, Goddess of battle and incitement,

Daughter of Ernmas, shape-shifting Goddess and great sorceress of the Tuatha de Danann.

May you hear this prayer and receive my offerings.

I honor you, Great Queen. Go raibh maith agat.

5.

An Mórrígan, hear my prayer.

Goddess of battle, satire and prophecy,

Goddess of sovereignty and sorcery,

I honor you, Great Queen.

May I hear your guidance as I do my work that needs to be done.

May I listen for what you communicate to me.

I will remain faithful to you, Goddess, and faithful to this path.

I give you my gratitude for the value that has been added to my life

And for your guidance that has helped me manage my challenges.

I will remain faithful to my work that is done for you,

Which in part, is internal work done on myself

For my healing, growth, and to reclaim my self-sovereignty.

May I achieve self-sovereignty and the strength that comes from it.

May I use the strength I gain to complete the tasks you bring me

And to achieve the personal goals that are important to me.

Thank you for this work you have brought to my life

And hold me accountable for.

May my efforts honor you, Great Queen.

Honor to you, An Mórrígan, Goddess that strengthens and incites.

Go raibh maith agat.

6.

An Mórrígan, Goddess of prophecy and battle,

Strategist that sees all and knows the ways of battle,

Goddess that plans with great skill,

And Goddess that brings great change, I honor you.

Hear my voice, shape-shifting Goddess.

Help me understand the ways I can be useful to you.

May I have clear direction as I complete my tasks

And work towards my goals.

May I do well with the projects you give me.

May I grow in skill as I invest my energy and effort.

May the work we do together honor you

And may I value the ways I am able to contribute.

Great Queen, I give you my efforts as an offering.

May they honor you.

Powerful and unconquerable, An Mórrígan,

Thank you for your time and for hearing my prayers.

Go raibh maith agat.

7.

Hear my voice, An Mórrígan, Goddess of sovereignty, incitement, and prophecy.

Hear my prayer and receive the offerings I bring to you.

Watch over my progress, Great Queen.

May I be disciplined with my studies and motivated with my self-work.

May I have wisdom as I invest in my growth.

May I engage only in the battles worthy of me, and those that I am ready for.

May I embrace change as it comes into my life

And may I understand my circumstances with clarity.

May I accept when changes are necessary for my growth.

May I hear and understand your guidance, An Mórrígan, as you provide it.

May I keep to my daily tasks and devotions faithfully and with gratitude.

With intention and self-governing, may I follow this path with purpose.

Thank you for the safety and abundance I experience in my life.

Honor to you forever, Great Queen. Go raibh maith agat.

8.

An Mórrígan, Goddess of battle and sovereignty,

Hear my voice as I offer this prayer.

May I learn how to best care for myself,

So that I have the energy and the resolve

To finish my tasks to completion,

And to your satisfaction.

May safety and peace stay with me in my mundane life.

May I make the choices that bring me the most benefit

And may I be responsible for them.

May I live my life honorably.

My deepest gratitude to you, An Mórrígan.

I honor you, Great Queen.

You have my devotion and my service as we work together.

Go raibh maith agat.

9.

Honor to you, An Mórrígan. Great Queen, I call to you.

Hear my prayer and receive my offerings,

Goddess that incites the warriors to face their battle.

Call me to my own battles, Goddess, when I'm ready to face them.

May I have the will to engage in the battles on the path laid before me.

May I be persistent in my efforts and achieve victory.

May I have the strength to stand for what is important

And the flexibility to experience growth in my understanding.

May I be faithful to do my internal work.

May I dig deeper into myself with unflinching honesty,

And despite the worthiness or unworthiness of my past,

May I care for myself and seek my own healing.

May I support my own growth and believe in the possibilities of my potential.

May I act with honor and rightness as I do my work.

May I have peace in my heart and safety upon me.

May my actions and choices be aligned with rightness.

I honor you, Great Queen.

Go raibh maith agat.

10.

An Mórrígan, Goddess of sovereignty,

I call to you with my gratitude and respect.

Hear my prayer, Great Queen, and receive my offerings.

You expect study. May I study the lore with persistence.

You expect training. May I develop my skills that are of use to you.

You expect effort and work. May I be faithful to the ways I am able to contribute.

May I undertake the work that benefits me and supports others, Great Queen.

May I foster my own growth as I honor my commitments.

May I invest in my practice and our relationship, An Mórrígan.

May I hear you and follow your guidance.

As I do my part to support positive change in this world,

May I know which battles and causes I am called to

And may I find the ways I can effectively contribute.

Thank you, Great Queen, for hearing this prayer.

I honor you, An Mórrígan.

Go raibh maith agat.

11.

Honor to you, Great Queen. Hear this prayer.

As I rise to meet the challenges of this day,

Inspire courage in me, Mórrígu.

May I glean knowledge from my experiences

And stay grounded when faced with difficult situations.

May safety be with me and all belonging to me, An Mórrígan.

May I always be aware of the guidance you have given me,

And may I act accordingly. May I remain accountable for my choices.

May my actions be honorable and aligned with the growth I have achieved.

May I stay focused on the work and on the tasks you have given me.

May my actions support my own growth and, when possible,

May I have the opportunity to provide support for others.

May I be diligent with my self-care and be able to maintain my mundane needs,

So that I am able to focus on the work you bring to me.

Honor to you forever, An Mórrígan.

Go raibh maith agat.

12.

An Mórrígan, hear this prayer and hear all the prayers I give to you.

I am here for you, Great Queen. To do the work that you give me.

Powerful are the words that you speak, Mórríu,

Red-haired satirist, sorceress with fistfuls of blood.

May I hear your words and study them in the lore.

Shape-shifting Goddess who has appeared in the form of a crow,

Receive the offerings I give to you, on this day and all days.

I will continue to honor you, An Mórrígan,

I will offer you respectful veneration and bring you the best of my ability

To do the work in your name that you ask of me.

I will not fail to check in with you daily, Great Queen, while we work together.

May I hear your guidance and may I listen.

May I hear your instructions and take them to heart.

May I hear you when you call for me. May I complete the tasks you give me.

May I always feel your presence when you look towards me.

May I be present for you, Goddess. I am here for you, An Mórrígan.

Thank you, Great Queen, for this and for all you have aided me with

That has contributed to my safety and to my growth.

I hold the times that we spend together as sacred. I value your time.

Go raibh maith agat.

Honor to you forever, Great Queen.

13.

An Mórrígan, I call to you with respect and devotion.

I honor you, Goddess that chanted poems that urged her people to battle

As they fought against their enemies. Hear my prayer, Great Queen.

I ask for your guidance, so that I take the necessary actions

To support my progress as I walk this path.

May the way forward be clear and accessible to me,

And may I receive your guidance and direction if I get off track.

May I do all that I am capable of and see the potential within me.

In the times that my work becomes difficult, may I have the strength to carry on.

May I not hinder my own progress. May I focus on the task at hand

And build the skills that will support my efforts.

May I be successful with the tasks you give me

And all that you guide me to do in your name, An Mórrígan.

May I exist in the present so that I am aware, awake, and available.

May I find the support and resources I need. May I give support where I am able.

May I hold space when I need to and listen to my own voice as well as the voices of others.

May I remember to attend to my self-care so that I remain well.

May I act honorably as I do the work I have committed to you.

I honor you, An Mórrígan.

Go raibh maith agat.

14.

Honor to you, An Mórrígan. Hear my prayer, Great Queen.

An Mórrígan, Goddess whose pleasure is in mustered hosts,

You are present on the battlefield and the giver of victory.

You bring triumph to your warriors that you lead into battle.

You call your followers, those that work for you and with you,

To the work you require of them. May I do the work you require of me.

May my efforts support your work in whatever ways I am able.

May my motivations and actions be aligned with the work

You have called me to, for your purpose. May my efforts honor you.

May I hear your instruction and prompting as you guide.

May I be careful with what I commit to,

So that I always honor my word and meet your expectations of me.

May I not disappoint you, Great Queen.

Hear my prayer, An Mórrígan. May I do the work you've given to me in your name.

I will be faithful to all I have committed to. I am in your service, Great Queen.

Honor to you, An Mórrígan. Go raibh maith agat.

15.

Honor to you, An Mórrígan. Great Queen, hear my prayer.

The first task of this day has begun, with my rising and this prayer.

Thank you for safety through the night for myself and all I care about.

May safety remain with me and all belonging to me, Great Queen.

As I go about my work, may I have the strength and the resilience

To pull away from unnecessary distractions,

To focus on my commitments that have a worthy purpose,

And to act honorably in all things while fostering the connections

That are important to me, especially my daily practice with you, Great Queen.

Guide me to the support and resources I need to accomplish my tasks.

May I hear you guidance as you give it to me, An Mórrígan.

May safety be with me throughout this day, for myself and all belonging to me.

Honor to you, Great Queen. Go raibh maith agat.

16.

An Mórrígan, hear my prayer. I honor you, Great Queen.

Goddess of sovereignty that sang poems of incitement

And stole the blood from the heart of the enemy king,

I call out to you with my respect. Honor to you, An Mórrígan.

May I receive the gift of your incitement, in the times that I need it,

While I do the work your have given me, Goddess.

May I receive the gift of your guidance, in the times I have lost my way,

And may I return soundly on this path you have led me to.

May I receive the gift of your aid, as your faithful devotee,

If a need arises, for the safety of myself and those I care about.

An Mórrígan, I honor you this day and I will continue to honor you all of my days.

May I act honorably towards myself and towards others.

May I give no space to colonizing views that diminish myself or cause harm.

May I listen and hold space for those whose voices are not being heard.

May I find victory in my battles and success in my the work I do for you.

May I set aside time for our projects together and my devotions daily

And keep a pace that supports focus in my thoughts and wellness in my body.

Thank you for your time and your aid, Great Queen. I honor you, An Mórrígan.

Go raibh maith agat.

17.

An Mórrígan, I honor you. Hear my prayer, Great Queen.

I dedicate this day to you and to the work that is waiting for me.

May I set my focus on my tasks. May my efforts be timely and honorable.

May I have patience with my progress. May I remember all I have accomplished so far.

May I keep my devotion in my thoughts and in my heart.

May I accomplish my goals that I have set for myself

And not become discouraged by any setbacks I may face.

May I complete my self-work and self-care,

And all the tasks I have committed to you with a good spirit.

May I not become overwhelmed, and in the times that I do,

May I find my grounding and nurture my peace within.

I honor you, An Mórrígan, and I value our journey together and our relationship.

Thank you for your time and your efforts on my behalf, Great Queen.

May I accomplish all you expect of me, Goddess.

May I not disappoint you.

Go raibh maith agat.

18.

An Mórrígan, I call to you with gratitude and respect.

I will embrace your call and the work you have given to me.

May I bring value to causes worthy of my effort and attention.

May I have clarity in my actions and intentions.

May I have triumph in my personal battles and the causes I battle for.

May I remember that my path asks a lifetime of service and resolve

In the ways I am able to contribute.

From the point where I stand today, may I live my life with rightness

To the best of my abilities, and with sincere effort.

May I show consideration to myself, to the individual lives of others,

And to the communities I am a part of.

May I recognize the opportunities to contribute,

And may I have the wisdom, skills, resources, and capabilities to do so successfully.

May I do my work honorably and may my efforts honor us both, An Mórrígan.

I honor you this day, Great Queen. I will honor you, Goddess, all of my days.

May safety and your guidance be with me, always.

Go raibh maith agat.

19.

An Mórrígan, hear this prayer. I honor you, Great Queen.

May I have the strength and will, with rightness and with resolve,

To accomplish my purpose and my work, Great Queen.

With your guidance, may I complete the inner work that will benefit me

And help me face the unresolved traumas that I need to address

So that I can move forward in my life in a healthier place.

May I carry myself well into the dark of my own memories and sit with my fears

Until I have resolved them. May I sit with my anger and rage until I understand them.

May I work through my traumas, and see every truth within myself.

May I find healing and self-sovereignty. May I awake. May I rise to my battles and face them.

May I remember, Great Queen, that no one is coming to save me

From doing the work I need to do, from seeing the hard truths about myself,

And from taking accountability for my own life.

An Mórrígan, may I embrace that my work will always be present.

May I find the discipline to accomplish my daily tasks to completion

And to complete as much progress as I can in this lifetime with your guidance.

May my efforts honor you, An Mórrígan. You have my loyalty always.

Goddess of incitement, battle, sovereignty, and prophecy,

I am faithfully invested in the work you give me.

Great Queen, may I be responsible to care for the needs of my body

And my well-being as I do the work I have been given. May safety stay with me.

Honor to you always, An Mórrígan. Go raibh maith agat.

20.

Great Queen, I call to you with respect. Goddess, you are welcome here.

Thank you for hearing my prayers and for your time we spend together.

Great Queen who has guided me through the facing of my traumas

And the steady rebuilding of my life, I honor you.

I come to you with devotion, Great Queen.

I will say your name with honor and remember your great deeds, An Mórrígan.

You took the form of different animals: eel, wolf, heifer, and crow.

You defended your people by weakening the Fomorian king with magical injury,

That the enemy king could not escape,

By stealing the blood from his heart and his kidneys of valor.

Prophetic Goddess of power and might, eternal and unfathomable Mórrígu, I honor you.

An Mórrígan, your prophecies have seen a future of peace and one of despair

And your people battle for the better future of this world.

As a Goddess of sovereignty, you have led me to the path of self-sovereignty.

May I defend my self-sovereignty and the self-sovereignty of others.

May I hold space for the voices that are not being heard.

May I see how to support the better future of this world.

May my actions be honorable and just. May I do the work to support own my healing.

May I have the wisdom and your guidance to know how to contribute my efforts.

Great Queen, thank you for hearing my prayers and for receiving my offerings.

Go raibh maith agat.

21.

An Mórrígan, hear my prayer.

Honor to you always, An Mórrígan, Goddess of battle and sovereignty.

I ask for your support as I continue my journey.

May I strengthen my own voice while still listening to the voices of others,

And may I do the work needed on myself for my own healing.

Goddess of battle and sovereignty,

You who inspire others to rise and defend their own sovereignty,

May I grow in strength and wisdom as I face my own battles.

May I value and defend my own sovereignty over myself

And put forth the effort to be self-governing,

With full accountability and responsibility for my life and my choices.

May I attain my self-sovereignty and never let it be taken from me.

Honor to you, Great Queen.

May I be honorable and just in all things. May I know the way to act with rightness.

May I understand and be aware of my motivations.

May I have your guidance when making hard choices.

May I live my life with focus, purpose, and faithfulness to the work you've given me.

I thank you for your time, An Mórrígan, and for your guidance and presence in my life.

May I invest in our relationship, Great Queen. May I be faithful to my daily practice.

May I share my time with you as we work together.

Honor to you forever, Great Queen. Go raibh maith agat.

22.

An Mórrígan, mighty Goddess of sovereignty and battle,

Hear my prayers this day and all days that I come to you.

Receive my offerings, Great Queen.

I honor you, shape-shifting goddess that can become all things at will.

I honor you satirist never to be crossed, poet with words of magic and power.

Honor to you, sorceress that rained fire and blood on the enemies of your people

And sent rain and fog to hinder them. I honor you, great prophetess that sees all.

Thank you for the work you have brought to me, Great Queen,

And for the work that we do together.

May I have a sense of resolve as I go about my daily tasks.

May I structure my goals with clarity and be flexible to the needs of the day.

May the vision for what I want to accomplish remain in my focus,

So that my motivation does not wane.

May I remember that every day I have another chance to make worthy choices,

To invest in my own growth and healing,

And to invest in my self-care, in all the ways my well-being requires.

As I direct my efforts inward, may my self-work be paired with self-love.

Honor to you, Great Queen. May I honor you with my efforts.

Thank you for your time, An Mórrígan.

Go raibh maith agat.

23.

An Mórrígan, hear my prayer. Great Queen, I honor you.

Thank you for safety through my travels, guidance in my interactions,

And for the lessons learned this day.

As this day is coming to an end,

May I examine my experiences,

So that I can put any knowledge learned from today to use in the future.

May I care for myself and rest. May I rest safely and soundly,

And may tomorrow may I be prepared to begin my work again.

I honor you, An Mórrígan. Thank you for your support and your guidance.

Thank you for this work you've given to me and this path I am on

That has contribute so much to my growth and well-being.

Honor and respect to you always, Great Queen.

Go raibh maith agat.

24.

Honor to you, An Mórrígan.

Hear this prayer, Great Queen that is present on the battlefield,

Watchful of the battle, and leading her people to victory.

Great queen, I honor you now and I will honor you tomorrow,

I will honor you the day after and the day after that as well,

And throughout this life.

I will be faithful to my daily practice and all I have promised you.

I will come to you daily with prayers and offerings.

I will do the work you give me.

Thank you for the experiences I have had on this path.

Thank you for this path that has given me the means and motivation

To live my life with sincerity and intention.

May I hear your guidance, An Mórrígan, when your direction is required.

May I hear you and may I understand.

Thank you for the work I have done so far to support my growth and healing.

With your guidance and support, may I find success with my work.

I will not neglect the promises I have made to you, Great Queen. I will be diligent.

Thank you for your time and for hearing this prayer, An Mórrígan.

Thank you for this work that we are doing together.

Go raibh maith agat.

25.

An Mórrígan, the Great Queen that resides in the Otherworld,

Hear my prayer, Goddess. May I understand how to live a life of honor and rightness.

May I become resilient to the impulses that would bring me dishonor,

May I not make my decisions based on fear, but through reason.

May I recognize any indoctrination that is harmful to me

And be able to dismantle it. May I examine my thoughts honestly.

May I never cease in my desire to live an honorable life.

May I not be half-hearted in my efforts or be neglectful towards my agreements.

May I never be absent when you call for me, Great Queen.

May I listen for you and be available to you.

I thank you for your support and guidance, mighty An Mórrígan.

Honor to you forver, Great Queen.

Go raibh maith agat.

26.

Honor to you, An Mórrígan. Hear my prayer, Great Queen.

Goddess of prophecy and sovereignty, I call to you with respect.

May I be mindful to the needs of the communities I am a part of.

May I appreciate the contributions of others and support their work.

May I give hospitality when it is called for, and remember the importance of it.

May I become skilled in communication, to be able to express my needs

And to be able to understand the needs of others. May I listen with respect.

May I hear and consider the advice of leadership and those that are more experienced

On this path, while remaining true to our relationship together, An Mórrígan.

May I develop my skills that benefit the work that you give me.

May I foster my spiritual relationships with the earth and my ancestors

And spend time nurturing my own spirit. May I listen to what inspires me.

May I remain committed to my studies of the Irish lore.

May I rightfully invest in myself, care for my needs, and rest,

So that I am better able to be of service to you, and to be useful to you,

May my self-care become a priority in my life.

I offer the time and effort spent on my studies and development to you, as an offering.

May it honor you, An Mórrígan. Honor to you forever, Great Queen.

Go raibh maith agat.

27.

An Mórrígan, I honor you.

You who defended your people by sorcery

And gave incitement before and during battle.

Hear my voice, Great Queen.

May it honor you, An Mórrígan, when I set my hands to the work you've put before me,

And complete the work I have agreed to.

Great Queen, you who took the kidneys of valor from the enemy king

And gave fistfuls of blood as the evidence of your act,

May I honor my commitments to you with rightness.

May I continue onward on this path through my life

And appreciate every experience that contributes to my growth.

An Mórrígan, ancient and powerful Goddess, I honor you.

May I find triumph in my battles,

And success with my work both external and internal.

My give you my fealty, Great Queen, while we work together

May I honor my time in this life and be productive with it.

May I reach deeply within myself, when needed,

And find the resolve to complete my tasks.

Honor to you, An Mórrígan. Great Queen, you have my loyalty and devotion.

Go raibh maith agat.

28.

Honor to you, An Mórrígan. Honor to you this day and all days, Great Queen.

Goddess of sovereignty, I call to you with respect and devotion.

As days pass, may I grow to be the person I believe I can be.

May I reach my potential as we work together.

May I build my strength and skills to aid the causes I believe in.

May I be willing and able to bring solidarity to the good fight

And stand beside those holding space for justice,

Beside those that defend the sovereignty of all people,

And beside those that challenge oppression in this world.

May I carry on with my efforts, Great Queen.

May I become more skilled in the ways I am able to contribute,

And may I contribute in every way that I am able.

May I support the work of others in the pagan community.

An Mórrígan, I commit to do the work that you bring to me - the work to do within myself,

Especially that which creates beneficial changes in my actions and mindsets.

At the end of each day, and whenever needed, may I rest.

May I be encouraged by whatever amount of work I accomplish,

No matter how humble, as long as I am making progress and keeping to my daily practice.

An Mórrígan, I honor you this day and I will honor you all of my days.

May my acts of devotion honor you. I offer them to you with devotion.

Go raibh maith agat.

29.

Great Queen, hear my prayer. May my words honor you, An Mórrígan.

I call out to you, Goddess, to thank you for your guidance in the times I have needed it.

Thank you for the tasks, and the challenges that have brought me growth.

Thank you for the ongoing work you will bring me, may I embrace it.

With honor and rightness, may I give my efforts faithfully to the work you bring me.

An Mórrígan, I understand that the work is never completed on this journey,

May I strive to complete each task to your satisfaction,

And may I meet each day with purpose.

Thank you for helping me build my ability to focus, calmly and clearly, at the task at hand.

I will faithfully keep to this path you have led me to,

This path that has added so much benefit to my growth and my life.

I honor you and I thank you, An Mórrígan.

May I have the resources needed to achieve my goals

And to maintain my mundane needs while we work together, Great Queen.

Thank you, An Mórrígan, for your support and your guidance.

Honor to you, Goddess of sovereignty and battle. Honor to you forever, Great Queen.

Go raibh maith agat.

30.

An Mórrígan, I honor you. Hear my prayer, Great Queen,

Honor to the changes you bring, Goddess.

You created change with strategy and cattle raids,

With incitement, prophecy and power,

And with the strategies that would aid your people in battle.

You have guarded the land by guarding fit rulership and the rightness of kings.

You see all born on the battlefield, you see the death and the valor.

Honor to you, An Mórrígan, Goddess of sovereignty and battle.

I am in your service, Great Queen, working for you and with you.

May your strategy bring great change in my life,

May change shape me for all that is necessary for my growth and healing.

May I find my strength. May I find valor in my own battles,

In the ways that valor would have meaning to me.

May I stand, incited, to face my battles when they come.

May I rise, awakened, and raise my voice.

With my loyalty and devotion, I honor you.

Thank you for the bringing of great change to my life, An Mórrígan.

Thank you for the changes you are bringing to this world.

Honor to you forever, Great Queen.

Go raibh maith agat.

31.

An Mórrígan, hear my voice. Goddess of sovereignty, I honor you.

As we work together and build our relationship,

May I do the work you give me,

And be diligent with my internal work.

May I achieve the potential you see within me, with your guidance.

Great Queen, may I continue my work with constancy,

With steadfast commitment and honorable action,

And honor the commitments we have agreed to together.

As I put forth the effort required to live a life aligned rightness,

May I hold accountability as sacred.

With your guidance, may I achieve the the growth I need

To stand in the power of my self sovereignty. May I live fearlessly and thrive.

For as long as we work together, An Mórrígan, be it for the rest of my life,

I will continue to do the work that you bring me, with respect.

I will continue on this path and may my actions honor us both.

Thank you for your guidance, Great Queen, may it help me stay in safety and wellness,

And become effective in what I'm trying to accomplish in this lifetime.

An Mórrígan, I honor you today, tomorrow, and for the rest of my days.

May I live a long life of faithful devotion to you.

My loyalty to you always, Great Queen. Honor to you forever, An Mórrígan.

Go raibh maith agat.

## Prayers of Invitation to Build or Deepen Relationship

32.

Honor to you, An Mórrígan, Goddess that brings incitement

To warriors and kings before the battle. I call to you, Great Queen. Hear me.

Goddess that brings the necessary battles that lead to change, I welcome you.

I call to you with respect and an offer to work together, Goddess.

Great Queen, consider the skills I have to offer and what work I can do for you.

Goddess, I know the work you bring will lead to the growth and changes I need in my life

To take back my freedom, and to become self-governing and self aware,

To find my strength and live honorably, to become accountable and self-sovereign,

And to face the battles that I have in my life.

Shape-shifting goddess, Mórrígu, I honor you with respect.

May I build a daily practice that suits us both, An Mórrígan,

One that gives us the space to build our relationship and work together

While still respecting our boundaries.

May I listen effectively, Great Queen, for the ways you speak to me.

May I give you the time and devotion you deserve.

I honor you, An Mórrígan.

Go raibh maith agat.

33.

An Mórrígan, Goddess renowned for sorcery, satire and prophecy,

I honor you.  I ask that you hear my prayer and receive my offerings, Great Queen.

With daily devotions and study, may our relationship grow stronger.

May I be able to support sovereignty in myself and others in whatever ways I can.

I choose the myself and I desire to build my strength.

I call out to you, Goddess, and ask that you help me build it.

Guide me through the changes I need to undertake in my life, An Mórrígan.

Guide my through my challenges and the battles I must face, Great Queen.

I thank you for your guidance and your direction.

See me An Mórrígan. Let us build on our relationship and work together.

See what work I can aid I can aid you with, Great Queen,

May I be of use to you. I am loyal and I am here. See me, Mórrígu.

Show me the ways you want me to work with you,

And let use continue our journey together.

Goddess of sovereignty and incitement, An Mórrígan, I honor you.

Go raibh maith agat.

34.

An Mórrígan, shape-shifting goddess of unmatched power,

I have felt your call and I am here, Goddess.

What is the work you have for me?

May I be guided to the ways that my efforts would be useful to you.

I call out to you, unconquerable Mórrígan, seeking connection with you,

To invite a deeper relationship together.

Let us work together, Mórrígu. Show me the way to reclaim my sovereignty

In all the places it is lacking in my life.

I will do the work to have a deeper and healed relationship with myself.

May I find the forgotten parts of myself that are calling me to find them.

With your guidance, may I be able to reclaim all of myself, An Mórrígan.

If you wish to work with me, I am ready to do the work you give me, Great Queen.

I call out to you, An Mórrígan. Hear me, Goddess. I am here.

May I find the ways to support positive change in this world,

And engage in the worthy battle for myself, to face the battle within.

Honor to you always, Great Queen.

Go raibh maith agat.

35.

An Mórrígan, Goddess of sovereignty, hear my prayer.

I give you honor and respect, Great Queen.

As I seek to build a stronger connection with you,

May I construct a daily practice that honors you and works well for us both.

May I understand where I need growth and healing within myself

And invest in that healing. May I learn to honor myself with self-care,

So that I am better able to do the work I need to do.

May I learn. May I find the right resources that will support me on my path.

May I study the lore with patience and contemplation.

May my inner journeys find you. May I listen and understand. May I learn.

May my path lead me to where I need to be.

May my eyes stay open and may I act with rightness and honor.

May I be instructed in the ways of right action – to learn what rightness is

And may my actions become aligned with honorable choices.

Honor to you, mighty Goddess of battle and sovereignty, of prophecy and change.

Honor to you, Great Queen.

Thank you for your time and for hearing this prayer, An Mórrígan.

Go raibh maith agat.

36.

An Mórrígan, hear my prayer.

I honor you Great Queen, Goddess of battle and sovereignty.

Giver of battle poetry and incitement before the battle, I honor you.

Giver of prophecy, satire, and wielder of magic,

You are the incitement of warriors and bringer of change.

You are the sacred claiming of sovereignty at all costs,

Reclaimed by those that work for it,

And develop strength, wisdom, and courage found deep within.

Hear me call to you, An Mórrígan. See me, Great Queen.

Guide me on this path to achieve self-sovereignty.

May I find my authentic self while we work together.

The work is what I offer, and whatever tasks you bring me,

done to the best of my ability, while we work together.

I offer my loyalty, my sincere effort, devotion, and offerings of time and effort.

Hear me, Great Queen.

With my deepest respect for you, An Mórrígan, I honor you.

Go raibh maith agat.

37.

An Mórrígan, I honor you.

Washer at the ford, battle-crow, satirist, sorceress,

Shape-shifting goddess that comes in many forms,

Goddess of battle and sovereignty, hear my prayer.

Hear my desire to take our relationship to the next level

And work together, with you as the deity I work for and work with.

Hear my commitment to do work that you give me -

With the skills you find within me, that will be useful to you.

May I be one more set of hands to join the many that work for your causes,

To bring change. May my voice be one more voice to join in the good fight

To support community, the land, rightness, and self-sovereignty.

May I aid you in your great work, even in some small way,

To support your strategies that come together to bring great change.

I honor to you, An Mórrígan.

Go raibh maith agat.

38.

Mórrígu, greatness of wealth and springs of craftiness,

Shape-shifting Goddess, I call to you. Hear my prayer.

Honor to you, Great Queen.

In studying your lore and learning about you, An Mórrígan, I desire to learn more,

And I invite you, Great Queen, for us to build a stronger connection

And to build a relationship together. Let us work together for my growth.

Show me how I would be useful to you, Great Queen. I will do the work you give me

To the sincere best of my ability.

See me where I am and the work that I am already doing.

May you see my potential within.

May you see the intentions to respectfully build a relationship with you

And my desire to honor you, An Mórrígan.

May I build upon the work I am doing already.

Consider me, Great Queen. I invite you. I seek you.

Go raibh maith agat. An Mórrígan, I honor you.

39.

An Mórrígan, mighty sovereignty goddess of Ireland, hear my prayer.

Respectfully I call to you, Mórrígu. Share some precious time with me, Goddess,

To see the ways my efforts can be of use to you.

Look into me, if you wish, and see what potential lies there.

I have a desire written in my heart for a deeper relationship with you.

Come see what I have to offer you, Great Queen. See me. Hear me.

I ask of you, An Mórrígan, to consider my invitation of collaboration,

And of my own devotion, Goddess.

Great Queen, my offer is to be of service to you - to do work for you as you call for me.

With loyalty and respect, with sincere effort, with faithfulness, and with devotion,

I honor you, An Mórrígan, and I thank you for your time.

I honor you, unconquerable and eternal,

Boundless and unfathomable, An Mórrígan.

Go raibh maith agat.

40.

Great Queen I call to you. Goddess, hear my prayer.

Shape-shifting Goddess of unmatched power,

Satirist and sorceress never to be crossed,

I call to you with the greatest of respect.

May I invest in our relationship daily,

and reach out with offerings and devotion.

With resolution and insight, may I continue to learn as I study and reflect.

May our relationship deepen, An Mórrígan.

I invite greater responsibility to do the work that you have for

And to move towards a long-term commitment together.

Guide me as we build our relationship together, An Mórrígan.

May I hear you and follow your guidance. May I study and prepare

For the work that you will bring me, and the work we will do together.

May no intruders be allowed to interfere during this sacred time,

As we consider each other and as we connect together.

May I know which battles are mine to take on,

And which battles do not deserve my efforts.

Go raibh maith agat. I honor you, Great Queen.

41.

An Mórrígan, shape-shifting Goddess of incitement and battle, of prophecy and sorcery,

Hear my voice. Great Queen, with respect and in devotion, I call to you.

See the struggles I have risen up against and have fought in my lifetime.

See the future battles I will need to rise up against.

May I face the battles within and challenge myself,

And focus on my own healing and growth.

I invite you, An Mórrígan, to lead me to work you have for me.

May I help support positive change in this world, in whatever ways I am able.

I invite you to the altar space I have set up for you, whether or not I am present.

It is your space, your space in my home, and you are also welcome throughout.

I look forward to the work we will do together, to seeking and the study,

And to the victory in battle, no matter how long the journey.

May I learn to see my own potential on my personal battlefield

And my ability to rise up despite any struggles that may come.

May I be safe in all things as I do the work you have given me, Great Queen.

May I walk this life with honor and rightness.

Goddess of sovereignty, may I embrace and defend my own sovereignty,

Throughout my life and until the end of it.

Go raibh maith agat. Great Queen, I honor you.

42.

An Mórrígan, hear my prayer.

Irish Goddess of sovereignty and battle,

Defender of the land, defender of the sovereignty of the people,

Hear me calling out to you, An Mórrígan.

See me. I am here. This calling I have felt led me to a path

That leads to you, An Mórrígan.

Great Queen, my desire is to work together, to work for you,

And to integrate, heal, and honor the shadow-self buried deep within me

In order to find my strength.

Whatever usefulness I have for you, Goddess, I will rise to meet the challenge.

May I have a clear understanding of the work you will ask of me.

May I honor you as we build our relationship. I will be available to you

And I will devote time daily to spend with you. I will study and research your lore.

Shape-shifting Goddess, of incitement and battle, of prophecy, I honor you.

Hear me as I invite a deeper connection between us, An Mórrígan.

May I foster the relationship we are building

And the strength of the communication between us.

Thank you for your time and for hearing my prayer, Great Queen.

Go raibh maith agat.

43.

An Mórrígan, Goddess of battle and sovereignty, I honor you.

Goddess, your strategy reaches long into the folds of time

And creates great change.

Your strategies are unknown to me, Great Queen,

But with your direction, may I help you with them

In whatever ways I am able, no matter how humble.

May I find my place among your army, whether on the battlefield,

Or on the supportive sidelines, may I be of service and use to you.

May my efforts be persistent and sincere,

And may they be worthy, Great Queen.

An Mórrígan, May my efforts be valuable to you. I dedicate them to you as an offering.

In the ways I am able, I will support your worthy causes and battles.

May I support the changes you bring to this world, Great Queen,

And experience change in my life as we work together.

I honor you, An Mórrígan.

Go raibh maith agat.

44.

Honor to you An Mórrígan, shape-shifting Goddess.

You have taken the form of a black bird perched on a pillar-stone.

You fought in the forms of a wolf, an eel, and a red-eared heifer.

You've taken the guise of a crone blinded in one eye,

And the guise of a youthful daughter of a king.

Red-haired sorceress and satirist, Great Queen, I honor you.

I am here at your altar, offering to work in whatever ways

I would be most useful to you.

May we deepen our connection as we work together.

May our relationship grow stronger as time goes on,

And as I invest my efforts, both in myself and in the work I am doing.

I am here. I am here, Goddess. Hear me and see me.

May I understand the ways to honor you,

And how to best support beneficial changes, both in my life

And in the lives of others, as I am able.

I accept that there are changes that need to be made in my life,

May I embrace them so that rightness in my life can be had,

And so that honor in my life can be realized,

May I take on my responsibilities and my purpose profoundly.

May I live daily with both action and intention,

And in my own sovereignty.

Go raibh maith agat. I honor you, Great Queen.

45.

An Mórrígan, Goddess of sovereignty and incitement - the incitement of battle,

Goddess of strategy that brings necessary change, and of prophecy, I honor you.

Thank you for this practice and our relationship we have built.

May this path continue in my life and extend further into my life.

As we work together, may I serve you in rightness and honor.

May I be steadfast and determined. May I be available to you, An Mórrígan.

May I give my efforts as an offering and may my offerings be worthy.

May I study the lore, and may I listen.

May I understand the information I gather as I learn.

I am loyal, Great Queen, I will remain faithful to all agreements

That we enter into together. I have remain devoted to you.

I give you honor and my assurance that I will continue with the work you give me.

I offer you praise, shape-shifting Goddess. I welcome you.

I invite you into my home, my life, and to have a deeper connection together.

I invite the work you bring to me. I invite your guidance, An Mórrígan.

I invite your direction on the work I am doing.

I invite hearing the hidden and difficult truths about myself

And experiencing change in my life as needed for my growth.

Mighty Goddess, I honor you and I thank you, Great Queen.

Go raibh maith agat.

46.

Hear my prayers, An Mórrígan. Honor to you, Great Queen.

I welcome you. I invite you, Goddess.

Great crow on the battlefield observant of the battle and sees all.

Goddess that speaks prophecies with power, I honor you

I reach out to you, Great Queen, with devotion and respect.

I welcome the opportunity to work together more closely.

May we connect on a deeper level. May I work to build our relationship.

Goddess of incitement, giver of battle poetry,

Giver of words igniting courage, valor, and when needed, fury,

Bringer of change, Defender of sovereignty,

Yours is the sorcery woven - Yours is the battle won.

Sacred is the sovereignty that the battle is fought for.

May triumph and sovereignty beget peace.

Yours are battle, magic, satire, prophecy,

Sorcery, shape-shifting, incitement,

And the bringing about of great change.

Yours is sacred sovereignty, An Mórrígan.

I honor you, Great Queen. An Mórrígan, I say this prayer as an invitation.

I will be responsibility for the work for you have for me.

May I receive it as I am ready and able to accomplish it.

Thank you, Great Queen, for your time and for hearing me.

Honor to you, An Mórrígan.

Go raibh maith agat.

47.

An Mórrígan, hear my prayer. Goddess of sovereignty, I honor you.

Thank you for the relationship we have built together so far.

Great Queen, I invite you into my life,

To deepen our connection together, and when you believe I am ready,

To begin the work that you would have for me.

May I have your guidance in my life.

I offer you my fealty, devotion, loyalty,

And to do the work you give me with sincere effort and consistency.

I will study and I commit to a daily practice as we work together.

Shape-shifting Goddess, An Mórrígan, hear my prayers and promises within them.

I will bring you daily offerings of devotion.

I will do work as I am able to support my growth on this path.

I offer committed relationship, An Mórrígan.

I am your devotee, Great Queen, now and as long as you will have me.

May my efforts be worthy offerings dedicated to you, An Mórrígan.

May I be worthy of the work you have for me and may I be successful in it.

You have my loyalty always, Great Queen, and my deepest respect.

Honor to you, An Mórrígan.

Go raibh maith agat.

48.

An Mórrígan, hear my prayer. Receive my offerings, Great Queen.

I call out to you with respect, An Mórrígan,

And I desire to do the work you bring to me.

See me, Great Queen, may I be known to you.

Show me the ways I can contribute, what battle to take on,

And what work I can do that would be useful to you.

May I hear your guidance as we build our relationship.

Let us work together, Great Queen.

May I remember the weight of commitment, especially with you.

May I never break an agreement made with you.

May I recognize your communication unmistakably.

Great Queen, my intent is to build a respectful relationship and to live my life honorably,

And to complete all agreements I make with you as we work together,

My desire for myself is to heal and live a life of rightness,

One that is honorable and contributes positively to this world I am in,

And that supports my spiritual development.

I ask this in your name as I call out to you, An Mórrígan.

May we work together for our mutual benefit and build a lasting relationship.

Honor to you forever, An Mórrígan.

Go raibh maith agat.

**Prayers Asking for Guidance with Shadow Work**

49.

Honor to you, An Mórrígan, I ask that you hear my prayer.

As I start this journey into shadow work,

Help me know how and where to begin.

May I know how to crack open those buried doors

And pull away the shrouds that lie within me.

May I have access to any memory I need to remember. Guide me as I explore.

May I find the trauma I'm ready to face and follow that pain

As it moves down into my depths,

I will sit with shame, fear, and hurt, an unfiltered audience.

I will listen to it all, and feel it all, and give it the space it needs.

I will gaze into its depths with objectivity.

With compassion, down through each layer, I will acknowledge it.

When all has been said, been seen, and accepted,

Then carefully, with love, I'll allow it to dismantle, integrate, or be released,

Or whatever it needs to be at peace, so that I can be at peace.

I will talk to it. I will remember that it belongs to me and I will embrace it.

I will gain back everything within that was stolen from me.

I will stand in truth unashamed.

I know you cannot and will not do for me,

This shadow work that you have tasked me with,

But I ask that you help me begin the process. Honor to you, An Mórrígan.

May you be honored, Great Queen, throughout all time. Go raibh maith agat.

50.

An Mórrígan, hear my prayer.

Great Queen, Goddess of sovereignty, guide me in my efforts in shadow-work

And my own journey for self sovereignty.

See my efforts and direct me when needed.

Watch over me as I begin this work and delve into the traumatic memories,

The pain, the fear, the grief, the resentment, and my chaotic rage within.

Watch over me as I reach deeply into my experiences of this life.

May I do this work that is necessary for my healing.

May it contribute to my growth and my strength,

So that I can be prepared for the other work you have for me.

May this journey to self-awareness, self-acceptance, and self-love be unhindered.

May I hold this journey as sacred. May this journey into my shadow be blessed

As I work towards connecting with my genuine self.

May I stand whole and unafraid.

May I not fear what I find in my dark.

May I meet my hurt and anger with love.

Thank you, Great Queen, for hearing this prayer.

I honor you, always. Go raibh maith agat.

51.

An Mórrígan, Goddess of battle and sovereignty,

Great Queen, I honor you. Hear my prayer.

May I be shown the ways to journey into my shadow,

So that I can face all that I have wrestled with in my life.

May I have courage to face the fears that have tried to overcome me.

May I face all aspects of myself that exist within me, whether they are beneficial or not.

May I become fully aware of the hidden and difficult parts of myself.

May I become aware and work through through memories I have shielded myself from

And process the buried fear, anger, and grief,

So that I can find myself and move forward in my life

With acceptance, accountability, and reclaiming my self-sovereignty.

May healing happen throughout me, as I do this work to save myself.

May I do the work within to love the most rejected and abandoned parts of myself.

May positive changes come to my life. May I become my most genuine self.

May I prepare for the journey that waits for me.

May the internal work I do honor you, An Mórrígan, as it strengthens me.

Honor to you forever, Great Queen.

Go raibh maith agat.

52.

An Mórrígan, Goddess that brings the necessary battle that leads to necessary change.

Goddess that brings the path to victory, I honor you. Hear my prayer, Great Queen.

May I find the healing that waits beyond my pain.

Goddess of sovereignty, that restores right rulership to the land,

May I choose my own well-being and put forth the effort to invest in myself,

Especially in regards to my internal work.

May I bring my love inwards with acceptance to all of myself.

May I find and achieve my restoration as I integrate my shadow.

Great-Queen, guide me to the ways to accomplish that feat.

Goddess of sovereignty, help me see the changes that I need to bring to my life

In order to obtain self-sovereignty.

May I become prepared in every way for the work you have set aside for me.

May it honor you as it also honors myself.

I am here, An Mórrígan, and I will continue to do the work you lead me to.

Go raibh maith agat. I honor you, Great Queen.

53.

Honor to you, An Mórrígan. Hear my prayer, shape-shifting Goddess.

As I reach deeply within to myself, to do the inner work you have given to me,

May I see myself with honestly and view myself without judgment

As I come to understand the most painful times in my life and face them.

Whether hurt was done to me or hurt done by me, may I accept the truth fully

And with awareness and accountability. May I make reparations where appropriate.

May I give forgiveness where that choice is appropriate for me,

Including forgiveness to myself.

May I find peace with who I am, and with intention,

I will decide how to walk the remainder of my life.

May I move forward in my life and live honorably.

May I learn to seek out the quiet and find peace in the stillness.

May I hear your guidance, Great Queen, when you provide it.

Help me see what changes would support my healing in my life.

May I have wisdom with my choices as I take responsibility for my self-care,

As I do the work I need to for my well-being.

Thank you for your guidance as I do this work, Great Queen.

Your guidance is sacred to me. I will listen. May I hear you.

An Mórrígan, bringer of change and inciter before the battle, I honor you.

Go raibh maith agat.

54.

An Mórrígan, Irish Goddess of sovereignty and battle, hear my prayer.

I honor you, shape-shifting Goddess that can become all things at will.

I ask that you guide me on this journey through the depths of my inner self.

May I hear your guidance, Great Queen, on this journey, and may I listen.

As I do my internal work, may I see and address any survival mechanisms

That bring harm to myself or create harmful experiences for others.

As I walk the winding path throughout my shadow side,

May I meet my pain and my fear. May I meet my feelings of rejection and my rage.

May I meet my hopes and the desires of my heart that are unique to me,

And may I sit with my regrets and make peace with them.

May I uncover all things I had once buried for my survival.

May all things become known to me that are within my dark

And may I allow myself to offer it love.

Keep watch over my progress, An Mórrígan,

As I work to integrate my shadow and claim sovereignty over my own life.

May my efforts to gain self-sovereignty be successful.

Thank you for your help and your guidance, Great Queen.

I honor you forever, An Mórrígan.

Go raibh maith agat.

55.

An Mórrígan, hear my prayer. Great Queen, I honor you.

Goddess that incites battle, when battle is necessary,

See the inner battle I face as I work through the pieces of my life.

May it honor you as I work through this process.

May my efforts honor myself as I work towards my mental and emotional well-being

By not running from the shadow sides from myself.

May I acknowledge the places within that I run from,

And may I remember that acknowledging them doesn't give them power over me.

May I see all of myself with clarity and acceptance. May I send my acceptance inward

And take back my power over myself with self-sovereignty and choice.

May I reclaim responsibility over my overall health.

Not only for my own well-being, but so I build my strength

To increase my ability to do the work you give me and my overall usefulness to you.

May I learn the skills that will support my work.

May I train and prepare in the ways most beneficial to the work I will take on.

May I successfully do the work that you bring me, Great Queen.

May my efforts be blessed, as I do this work in your name, An Mórrígan.

You have my devotion and I give my gratitude to you.

My respect to you always, Goddess. I honor you.

Go raibh maith agat.

56.

Hear my prayer, An Mórrígan.

I honor you, mighty Goddess of battle and sovereignty.

May I work towards my self-sovereignty faithfully

And acknowledge all things with honesty,

Without denying truth to anything within.

May I find healing and strength through the inner work I undertake.

May I gain wisdom regarding myself.

As I gain my own sovereignty, may take the actions necessary

To hold space to support the self-sovereignty of others

And defend justice where I am able.

May I honor myself by living a life with rightness.

May I become rooted in a place of strength.

May I have the courage to embrace my whole self,

Including the least favorable parts of myself.

May I make honorable choices in my life with the full understanding of who I am.

May I walk this path, my journey, with my eyes wide open.

Go raibh maith agat. Honor to you, Great Queen.

57.

Hear my prayer, An Mórrígan, Irish sovereignty Goddess.

Goddess that incites before the battle and brings prophecy,

I am in your service, Great Queen. I honor you, An Mórrígan.

I ask that you support my goals that align with the work you have for me.

I ask for your guidance as I work to meet and integrate my shadow-self

For the wisdom, strength, and healing that comes from that.

See the inner work I am doing, Mórrígu. May my efforts by guided by you when needed.

With intention, may I take back the power of choice that in the past I had given away.

May I keep the connections I desire and cut the cords of attachment that do not benefit me.

May I acknowledge the relationships in my life that are not beneficial

And may I establish boundaries that are healthy for me.

May I move forward from those relationships constructively.

Thank you for your guidance in the times that I need it.

May I continue to work on myself with a sense of devotion.

While I do my shadow-work, may I understand clearly.

May I accept the profound realizations about my life as they surface.

May I have the courage to accept every truth that belongs to me.

I give my gratitude to you, An Mórrígan, Goddess of prophecy and sovereignty.

Honor to you forever, Great Queen.

Go raibh maith agat.

58.

An Mórrígan, hear my prayer. Great Queen, I honor you.

Mighty Goddess of prophecy, battle, and sovereignty,

Shape-shifting Goddess, whose fit abode holds

Perfect darkness and silence within its sacred walls, I call to you.

As I explore my darkness and seek out my silent places within,

May I linger as long as I need to and embrace it.

May I journey within as far as I need to and as far as I am able.

May I revisit as often as I need to - until I find peace within the darkness.

Watch over me as I do my shadow work, Goddess.

May I revisit the times of dishonor in my own life - times when my actions were unworthy.

May I take accountability and see the truth behind my intentions and my choices.

May I explore my feelings, thoughts, and actions without immediate judgment.

May I have the courage to be honest with those situations and my intentions.

May I be objective, thorough, and fearless while unpacking any trauma

I have done to myself or I have done to others.

May I dismantle what needs to be dismantled. Let me find the ways to give recompense.

If discussion is required, I will face it. If self-forgiveness is required, may I grant it to myself.

May I acknowledge that I am worthy of my love and my acceptance despite my past,

And grant it to myself when I'm ready.

With the promise of continuing to do the work needed on myself,

With acknowledgment and accountability, may I hold space for my truth.

May I live in rightness and do the work I need to do, as promised, in your name.

Honor to you, An Mórrígan. Go raibh maith agat.

59.

An Mórrígan, hear my prayer. Honor to you, forever, Great Queen,

Goddess of battle and sovereignty,

Giver of battle-poetry, incitement, prophecy, and sorcery,

I honor you, with loyalty and devotion.

I ask that you guide me with the work I set my hands to,

And the shadow work I have set my heart and intention to.

With study and journeying within myself,

May I gain the growth and healing I require, An Mórrígan.

May I become stronger and more aware as I do this work in your name.

As I heal alongside my shadow and keep what belongs to me.

May I work from a place that supports my growth

And is capable of supporting my authentic self.

May I become capable of offering support to the communities I am a part of.

May I be available to others that request my aid

Appropriate to what I can give.

Thank you, Great Queen. May this work that I do honor you.

May I make decisions based in rightness.

Honor to you, An Mórrígan.

Go raibh maith agat.

60.

An Mórrígan, sorceress of incredible power,

Great Queen present in battle, battle crow with watchful eyes, I honor you.

As I engage with my shadow self within, may I remain open to learn from it

And gain the wisdom that it provides.

May I have the strength to open all the doors locked deep within,

And unravel the damage done to me and that I have done to myself.

May I support the ways that I heal and foster existing as my genuine self

With the fear of judgment of others or rejection.

May I exist in my whole truth and discovery the hidden parts of my character.

May I open all the locked doors within and find the truths I've hidden from myself.

May I make choices with awareness to return every part of myself to rightness.

May I learn how to defend myself constructively. May I embrace my self-worth.

May I believe in my potential and not dishonor myself.

Guide me in these changes, An Mórrígan, to your honor and to my own.

Thank you for guiding me through this process, Great Queen.

May I become the strongest and most authentic version of myself

And may I become more capable of doing the work you give me

To do in your name, An Mórrígan. I thank and honor you, Great Queen.

Go raibh maith agat.

61.

An Mórrígan, hear my prayer. May I honor you well,

Irish goddess of sovereignty that brings justice

And shapes the environment the surrounds her followers

To cause the needed changes within them. I honor you,

Goddess that delivers incitement to her warriors to face their battles.

I ask you to give me incitement, Great Queen, if I fall away from my internal work.

May I be incited to carry on and reach deeper

When my shadow-work becomes difficult and uncomfortable.

May I remember the value that comes from this work.

May I embrace the understanding that this internal work never ends.

I will foster this agreement, for these changes that are coming, with myself.

I am worth it and I will foster, care for, and love myself.

Great Queen who gives incitement, guide me in the times I need it.

Provide me with your incitement when I am falling short of the effort I can truly give.

My service and devotion to you, An Mórrígan, with sincerity, loyalty, and love.

May I be strengthened as I do this work and ask every hard question of myself.

As I invest in myself and work through my trauma

May I awake to my unconscious patterns of self-destructive actions.

May I become self-governing and achieve self-sovereignty.

May I understand how to integrate my shadow into my conscious life.

May I address my triggers and the reasons behind them.

May I give myself the self-care I need.

Honor to you forever, Goddess of sovereignty and battle. Go raibh maith agat.

62.

An Mórrígan, honor to you, Great Queen of battle and sovereignty.

Honor to you, powerful sorceress and satirist.

Honor to you, prophetess of both victory and doom.

Thank you, An Mórrígan, for hearing me when I call out to you.

I admit my struggles with distraction in my life,

May they not take away from my investment in myself

Or the commitments I have made to do this shadow-work

And all other work I have promised for you.

Honor and gratitude to other that are doing their work for you,

May I support them as I am able. I respect the community of those devoted to you.

May I be directed, Great Queen, to the shadow-work I need to do.

Help me with your guidance, to gain direction and clarity in my life.

May I find the path to achieve self sovereignty

And work through all I need to become established in my work.

May I take the actions necessary for me to heal,

And give myself the self-care I need.

I am here for whatever truths I must face about myself.

May I explore the reasons why I deny myself the self-care I need.

Thank you for showing me that no one is coming to save me.

Thank you for showing me that I must carry the weight of my work

And that I am accountable to be faithful to it. May I be incited by your expectations.

Honor you, eternal Mór Ríoghain. Go raibh maith agat.

63.

Honor to you, An Mórrígan. Great Queen, hear my prayer.

May strength come to me in the days when every action is a struggle.

May I find encouragement in your guidance.

Help me know that I am worthy of the effort to do the self care I need to do.

May I see it as a form of self-love and as an act of devotion to both of us.

May I be faithful to give myself the self-care I need to carry on.

Thank you Goddess for helping me find the ways to support myself.

May I be effective with the work you have for me.

May I gain grounding from the experiences as I build.

May I learn from my mistakes and course-correct as needed.

May I have the courage to continually dig deeper as I look within.

When the work becomes overwhelming, may I remember

That I deserve this effort I am investing in myself

And that I deserve healing, self-worth, and to turn my love inwards.

During the course of this shadow-work, which will occur throughout my life

In life-altering ways that will evolve as I continue on this path, I will honor myself.

May I learn to trust myself as I shift my actions towards rightness and grow in confidence.

Thank you, Great Queen, for your help. Thank you for hearing this prayer.

Honor to you forever, An Mórrígan. Go raibh maith agat.

64.

Honor to you, An Mórrígan, sovereignty Goddess of Ireland.

Goddess, I have heard you calling me back to myself

And I have felt you watch my progress with a careful eye.

Goddess that expects much and is deserving of all, An Mórrígan, I honor you.

May I discover all of my truth that I have sequestered to my shadow.

I call back any memories I've hidden from myself. An Mórrígan, help me with this.

By the will of my own heart, by my bones, my flesh, my blood,

By the impulses of my nerves reaching throughout me, I call back the memories of my body.

I call back every experience, whether of joy or pain.

I welcome the knowledge of my whole truth.

May I do the work to undo every lie I've told myself, whether out of fear or to survive.

May my earth give back its buried bones.

May my skies give me back my tempest.

My my fire burn away the overgrowth

And my waters bring a flood that wash the remnants away.

May every hidden truth come to my remembrance.

I embrace my shadow-self with joy and love.

I seek to explore the darkest parts of myself with understanding.

May the Mórrígan bless this prayer and my efforts to do this work.

My devotion, loyalty, and gratitude to you, Great Queen.

I honor you. Go raibh maith agat.

65.

Hear my prayer, An Mórrígan. I give you my honor and respect.

Great Queen, you are known to call your devoted to their shadow-work.

I am one of your own,  An Mórrígan. See me, Great Queen. Know me.

May I uncover every reason I have ever felt trapped, isolated, or rageful,

And process it as needed. May I recount my experiences with honesty.

May I remember that while this work takes significant effort,

The results in my life will also be significant.

I will not collapse under the weight of my fears. I will face them.

I will thrive despite my challenges. I will celebrate my achievements.

I understand now, Mórrígu, that no one is coming to save me,

And I know now that no one needs to.

I can save myself.

I know you are with me, Great Queen. I am grateful to you.

Thank you, An Mórrígan. I honor you now

And I will honor you always. Go raibh maith agat.

66.

Hear my prayer, An Mórrígan. I honor you, Great Queen.

I offer my shadow-work as an offering to you, Great Queen.

May I face the secreted, forgotten, and the unknown

With courage and compassion.

An Mórrígan, in my heart

May my efforts follow my desire to be successful as I do my shadow-work,

And may my efforts serve me well.

I will follow the path that leads towards my healing and growth.

And I will take up my internal battles as they come.

Help me to recognize my self-destructive traits,

To search for the reasons I created or learned them,

And what situations fostered them.

May I see myself objectively and honestly.

May I be empowered with the understanding that I have choice over my life.

May I be empowered by the knowledge that choice

Comes with accountability and its own power.

Great Queen whose brings me to face my shadow within for the healing,

Strength, and wisdom that comes from that, may I find my shadow-self and learn from it.

May I integrate my shadow-self with my conscious self.

May I work towards becoming self-governing in all ways and at all times.

May I understand myself and find peace.

Thank you for your guidance, your time, and your support, Great Queen.

Go raibh maith agat.

67.

An Mórrígan, Goddess wise strategy and battle, I honor you.

Hear my prayer, satirist and sorceress whose power transforms.

You transformed ŧdras into a stream, and through shape-shifting,

You transform yourself at will. Your poetic incitement aided your people

In the times of battle and your sorcery wielded havoc on their enemies.

Honor to you, Great Queen. I reach out to you with my deepest respect.

Guide me as I examine what I need to do in my life and learn what my boundaries should be.

May I establish and understand what is healthy for me

And have the courage to defend the healthy boundaries I need in my life.

May I remain steadfast with my efforts towards self-sovereignty

And my work to integrate my shadow-self.

While I engage in this sacred process,  may I find the healing that waits for me.

May I be able face all truths within me and find the hidden aspects as well.

May I see beyond my own masks. May I see any truths I have run from.

May I face the root of my anger and my fears.

May I touch the wound and explore it. May I sit with the pain, examine it, listen to it,

May I reach down into the depths of that pain and beyond it to find the hidden within.

May I have persistence in the midst of my battles, An Mórrígan.

I will not forget my promises made to you, Great Queen.

Honor to you always. Go raibh maith agat.

68.

Hear my prayer, An Mórrígan. I honor you, sorceress and satirist. I welcome you.

I invite you into my shadow-work, in any way you wish to be included

And to be present with me, Great Queen. I ask for your guidance when I need it.

I dedicate my shadow-work to you, An Mórrígan,

May it honor you as it brings healing to me.

What lies in my depths, may I bring to my awareness,

So I can emerge a stronger and healed person and reclaim sovereignty over my life.

I will seek out any trauma I have denied a voice to.

May I not run from truth; may I not run from terror.

Guard me with your watchful eyes, as I become conscious of my shadow-self

And work towards healing and wholeness.

I thank you for your messages of guidance, Great Queen.

May I remember them. May I listen.

Honor to you, An Mór Ríoghain.

Go raibh maith agat.

69.

Honor to you, An Mórrígan. Hear my prayer, Great Queen.

In your name and for your purpose, Great Queen.

May the great changes you bring unfold upon this earth

And may I do my part by beginning with what needs to be changed within myself.

So I can effectively participate in the support of positive changes in this world,

The causes of justice, and a return to rightness in this world,

May I prepare myself by healing what is broken within me

And emerge strong and capable to do the work you give me.

May I do all that I can with rightness and courage,

the battles you have laid before your people and the changes you are invoking.

Great Queen, I will honor your call dutifully for all you see fit to give me.

May I see the reasons behind the suffering in my life,

Whether caused by my actions or by the actions of others.

May I be successful in my internal work and may I continue on its path.

Through this shadow-work I've undertaken,

May everything that is not easily seen, become known to me.

May I be successful with my efforts.

Honor to you forever, An Mórrígan.

Go raibh maith agat.

70.

An Mórrígan, hear my prayer. I honor you, Great Queen.

Sovereignty Goddess of Ireland, I thank you for charging me with this work

To change myself, to grow, to find my healing, and to reach my potential.

You have my eternal gratitude that you found me and brought me into your fold.

I will face all that lies within me with this shadow work. I will face my fears.

You have given me the call to do this internal work, to dig deep within myself,

To create a great change in my life, to reclaim my self-sovereignty,

And the call to become able to accomplish the work you have set aside for me.

May I embrace the most angry, hurt, and rejected parts of myself with compassion.

May I sit with the heartbreak, the fears, the rage, and the fears within my shadow-self.

May I never take for granted the power of my choice and may I use it.

May I remain aware of my accountability and call to honorable action in my life.

May I defend my boundaries and my voice. May I respect the boundaries and the voice of others.

May I take up the battle for my self sovereignty and defend it.

May I defend the rights of others to gain and maintain their own self-sovereignty.

Hold me in safety and rightness, An Mórrígan. Hold me to my word.

Great Queen receive my offerings, my effort, and may you always hear my prayers.

I am devoted to you and I will stay committed to the work I have agreed to.

I am your devotee, An Mórrígan. I am here for you. May I hear and heed your guidance.

Honor to you, ancient Goddess, battle-crow, sorceress, prophetess, satirist,

And She who sees this world holding the strategies for great and necessary change.

I honor you always, Great Queen. My loyalty to you forever, Goddess.

Go raibh maith agat.

## Prayers Asking for Help with Mundane Needs and Resources

71.

An Mórrígan, Goddess that brings battle-poetry, incitement, and necessary change,

Receive my prayers and the offerings I bring to you.

Hear my voice as I ask for your guidance and your assistance.

I call out to you, Great Queen, with appreciation and respect.

I am working steadily on the tasks you have given me,

And I will continue to be faithful to them and to you.

Great Queen, I ask that my financial circumstances be generous

And that I have security in my mundane life.

May I have enough money for my needs and also to be generous with others.

May I have enough to invest in the needs of my community.

If there is a more prosperous path of employment or undertaking,

May I have your guidance to become aware of it.

I will be responsible with what I am given.

May I find work that aligns with my ethics, my purpose, and my path.

Help me realize what path and actions to take.

I give you my promise that my focus will continue to stay

On the higher work, which is the work that you give me.

May my mundane life be financially stable,

So that I am not distracted by my financial needs.

I am grateful for your help with this, and all other matters, as I walk this path.

I honor you, An Mórrígan, Goddess of battle and sovereignty. Go raibh maith agat.

72.

Honor to you, Great Queen, mighty sovereignty Goddess of Ireland.

Goddess of battle and battle poetry. Goddess that brings change,

Thank you for the changes you have brought in my life,

And thank you for the work you have given me.

May my efforts honor you, Great Queen.

I ask that I have safety, security, and all the basic requirements

Needed for my well-being in my mundane existence as we work together, An Mórrígan.

I will not neglect the work I have promised to do for you.

May I have the time and resources to be effective with my work.

May I find the support I need in all things.

I take full responsibility for the promises I have made to you, An Mórrígan.

You have my devotion, Great Queen, and my loyalty.

May the needs of my mundane life be easily maintained,

And my life blessed with calm and abundance,

So that my focus is easily kept upon the work you have given me,

I ask these things in your name, An Mórrígan, with the understanding that the work

You bring is often constant and demanding. You are worthy of the work you ask.

I will continually give you my sincere efforts.

I will be responsible for my self care and to rest as needed.

May I be able to give you all that it is expected from me.

Hear my prayer, Goddess. I honor you and I thank you for your aid.

Honor to you forever, Great Queen. Go raibh maith agat.

73.

An Mórrígan, hear my prayer. I honor you, Great Queen.

May this home be a sanctuary to me, and my safety be assured

While I dwell in it. May I have safety upon myself and all belonging to me.

I will honor you, Great Queen, for as long as I draw breath in this lifetime.

May I live a long life that is dedicated to you throughout the years ahead of me.

May my home be a sanctuary of protection and peace.

May my home be blessed with safety,

And may I always have a place that I can call my home.

May I have security in my life and my shelter be secured, Great Queen.

Thank you for your aid and for hearing this prayer.

I honor you now and I will honor you always, An Mórrígan.

Go raibh maith agat.

74.

I honor you, An Mórrígan, shape-shifting Goddess.

Hear my prayer and my petition for your guidance, Great Queen.

May I invest in my health to be at my body's potential. May I thrive.

May I be guided to the treatments and doctors that will best support me.

May I be wise in my efforts for self-care.

Lead me to the knowledge I need for my well-being

And I will take responsibility for my actions that benefit my health.

May I always have access to clean water my body requires.

May I have access to healthy food, and may I be appreciative for it.

May I honor myself by investing in my physical well-being

In ways that align with my specific needs. May I rest when I need to

To care for myself and maintain my well-being.

I am in your service, An Mórrígan. May I diligently do the work that you give me,

As much as you feel I am ready for, and as much as I can safely handle.

Honor to you forever, An Mórrígan.

I thank you for your guidance and support.

Go raibh maith agat.

75.

Hear this prayer, Great Queen. Mórrígu, I honor you.

Goddess of sovereignty, incitement, and battle.

I have come to you with a request for your guidance

To find the most successful ways for my mundane needs to be met.

Help me find security in my life, An Mórrígan,

For the well-being of myself and those belonging to me.

An Mórrígan, I ask that I always have employment, whenever I desire it,

And that my employment aligns well with my path and my ethics,

And may it support my well-being. May I find the best employment that suits my needs.

May I be wise with where I choose to work and be successful there.

May I have the good fortune, favor, and capabilities needed to do well,

And I will be sincere with my responsibilities and my efforts.

So that I am not distracted by my mundane needs, may I have the mundane resources I need,

While I do the work you have given to me.

An Mórrígan, your work and my service to you is my priority.

May I and all belonging to me be safe, secure, and able to live in peace.

Thank you for your guidance and you aid with these requests, Great Queen.

I thank you for your support, Goddess.

Hear this prayer, An Mórrígan, and receive my offerings.

I am in your service, An Mórrígan. I am devoted to you, Great Queen.

Go raibh maith agat.

76.

An Mórrígan, hear my prayer. I honor you with devotion and loyalty in my heart.

May I have the resources and wherewithal to contribute and invest

In the needs of the community I live in and the greater community beyond.

May I have the abundance available to give from what I have

And provide easily for my family.

May I have the awareness to maintain a sense of responsibility as appropriate

For my own needs and the needs of my loved ones.

An Mórrígan, Goddess that I work with and work for,

May I have the resources to contribute to the needs of my community,

And to invest in the work in ritual tools, study resources, and physical offerings to give,

That help me to maintain this path I am on.

May I have resources to contribute to worthy causes that maintain guardianship

Over this world's land, sea, and sky and my I have wisdom to honor and support as I am able.

May I have resilience and resolve as I walk my path.

May I have the resources, energy, time, and capabilities

To contribute well and in a way that honors you, An Mórrígan.

May I add value where I am able, with your direction and guidance.

May I be a help to your communities I belong to.

May I be a benefit to and contribute in beneficial ways to the world around me.

May I have the resources to offer contributions that support positive changes in others.

I bring you the willingness to do the work to becoming a better version of myself,

Both for my own benefit and to be capable of the work you have for me.

Honor to you, An Mórrígan. Go raibh maith agat.

77.

An Mórrígan, guardian of the land and Goddess of sovereignty,

You engage the hearts of warriors through incitement and bring victory in battle.

You defend sovereignty and right-rulership, and therein wellness of the land.

Great Queen, I will give you my best efforts with the work you bring to me.

I ask that I possess the resources, energy, and time needed for my success.

I will give with whatever strength I have. May I rest when needed to invest in my well being.

May I have the wisdom to manage my resources well,

So I am able to be responsible for my mundane needs.

May I have security in my life, Mórrígu,

So that I can focus my attention on the work you have given me.

You have my assurance that I will continue to do the work

And that I will be faithful to it.

I thank you for your time, An Mórrígan. I honor you, Great Queen.

Thank you for the opportunities for personal growth and recovery

That you have brought to me in my life.

I am grateful for your guidance and aid when I have needed it, Goddess.

May I do all you expect from me with rightness and resolve.

May my efforts be useful to you and may they honor you.

You have my loyalty and my devotion, An Mórrígan. I honor you, Great Queen.

Go raibh maith agat.

78.

I call out to you, An Mórrígan, shape-shifting Goddess

And mighty strategist. I honor you. Great Queen, hear my prayer.

May I develop healthy boundaries that honor me

And may I have the wisdom to seek out any mundane support I may need.

May I be honest with myself in regards to my well-being.

May I become objective and observant,

And be aware if I'm not making my mental health a priority.

May I be directed by you, An Mórrígan, whenever possible

As I seek out what support and treatments will aid me,

And as I work towards achieving my personal best when it comes to my health,

May I have wisdom as I prioritize my needs.

May I hold myself as sacred and worthy of the care I need for my well-being,

And may I successfully win the fight for my care, if needed, in the face of my illness.

May I not become overwhelmed when trying to get help and support I need.

May I have the benefit of your guidance, Great Queen,

And be led to the healers, caregivers, and treatments most beneficial to me -

And may their doors burst open to welcome me, if needed.

May I take responsibility for my own health and well-being. May I rest when I need to rest.

May I listen to my body, find stability for my mind, and nurture my spirit.

When I am ill, may I recover quickly to return to the work you have for me.

Honor to you forever, An Mórrígan.

Go raibh maith agat.

79.

An Mórrígan, Goddess that gives prophecy

And poetic incitement before the battle, I honor you.

Hear my prayer, Great Queen. I wish to develop my skills

And strengthen my abilities. May I refine them

So that they better serve me with the work I'm doing for you.

May I be guided in the best ways to invest in my skill sets

And led to the tools and education that will support my efforts.

May I successfully increase the skills I'll use in the work I've promised to you.

Lead me to the teachers that I will benefit from the most.

May I find resources and support that will aid me with my efforts.

Great Queen, I dedicate my study and efforts to you as an offering.

Direct and guide me, Goddess. May I have success in my endeavors.

Honor to you always, An Mórrígan.

Go raibh maith agat.

80.

An Mórrígan, hear my prayer, Goddess. Receive my offerings, Great Queen.

May I return to your altar daily and spend time in prayer and peaceful study.

You are very welcome here, Goddess, throughout my home and my life.

May I reach my potential and have the security in my life while I do my work.

May my home be blessed with safety and peace, An Mórrígan.

May I have a secure space for my acts of devotions and my altar.

May I have a home that is free from harassment and intrusion,

And if, Great Queen, changes need to be made for that happen,

I am open to those changes. May I have your guidance.

As I grow in my awareness, may I see the gaps in my self-care.

I commit to being responsible for my care and giving the necessary effort for it.

May I find my best path for health in my body,

However that looks for this body I've been born into.

May I find my best path for the health of my emotions and my mind,

However that healing can best take place within me.

May I find the best ways to honor my own spirit and connect to the land, sea, and sky.

An Mórrígan, may I develop the best daily practices for my life

And be open to growth and change.

May I give as much hospitality to myself as I would give to another,

And may I have the space in my life to provide hospitality when it is asked of me.

I honor you, An Mórrígan. Thank you for hearing these prayers.

Thank you for your guidance and your aid, Great Queen. Go raibh maith agat.

81.

An Mórrígan, Goddess possessing power and might, hear my prayer.

Honor to you, Mórrígu that brings victory.

May you be honored by the offerings I bring and my devotional work.

May my prayers and spiritual work honor you.

May my meditations and journeys reaching out to connect,

Honor you, Great Queen. I will bring what I have to do the work you have for me.

May my efforts and contributions be useful and beneficial.

May my attempts to study prove fruitful and may my skills strengthen.

As time goes by, may my contributions increase as I become stronger and more skilled.

An Mórrígan, who has power indeed, who has stood fast, and is victorious,

I will honor you throughout this lifetime with loyalty and respect.

May my offerings be given with sincerity and remain worthy.

May I follow be guided through my creative process

When creating devotional items and may the effort and care I invest honor you.

May I find the communities where I share my support for others,

And where I can share my creativity and celebrate that efforts of other.

May I study successfully as I seek to improve my craft.

May I continue to have the means to undertake my devotional projects.

May my efforts honor you, An Mórrígan.

Honor to you forever, Great Queen.

Go raibh maith agat.

82.

Great and mighty An Mórrígan, I honor you, Great Queen.

I will be faithful to the commitments I have made with you.

Thank you for the work you give me, Great Queen.

May opportunities arise as I continue to develop

And as I do the work you give me with sincere effort.

I will be faithful to the guidance you have provided me.

I ask, so that I can stay focused on my work without distractions,

That my financial needs be easily met and my employment be easily kept.

May any debt I've incurred steadily fade away.

May my mundane needs be maintained and may I have security in my life.

I ask for your guidance involving any changes in my employment

And the management of my resources,

If that guidance is needed for my well-being.

Thank you for your time, Great Queen.

I appreciate your guidance, your aid, and the insights you give me.

I am devoted to you and I will be faithful to all we have agreed upon.

I honor you forever, An Mórrígan.

Go raibh maith agat.

## Prayers Asking for Protection

These are prayers asking for protection. Prayers can help, but they are not a substitute for getting mundane support, especially if you are concerned about your safety and security. While some of these prayers are asking for protection in a general way, most are written with the intent of asking for intervention for a specific need.

83.

An Mórrígan, Goddess that guards the sovereignty of the land,

Goddess that can bestow sovereignty and can remove it, I honor you.

Great Queen, I ask for your support as I claim sovereignty,

Over myself, my home, and all that belongs to me.

May I be a good steward of what I have

And may its safety be assured.

May I stay in possession of all that belongs to me

Until I choose to release it.

May my sovereignty over what is mine, remain mine.

With your help and your guidance,

May none be successful that try to harm me.

In you name, An Mórrígan , may safety and security be upon me

And all that has value to me.

I honor you, An Mórrígan.

Go raibh maith agat.

84.

An Mórrígan, hear my prayer. I honor you, Great Queen.

Sorceress and satirist of great renown,

You defended your people with sorcery in their time of battle.

You took the kidneys of valor from the king of your people's enemy

And weakened him. You gave evidence of your act with fistfuls of blood.

May your protection be on me, Great Queen,

And may my safety be assured to me as I walk this path.

Great Queen, I ask that no threats against me come to pass.

May no danger touch me. May no harm come against me.

May any attacks against me end with victory on my side.

Mórrígu, I ask for your protection to stay with me and all belonging to me.

Thank you for your aid, Goddess of battle and sovereignty.

When you call for me, I will answer. I will do the work that you ask of me.

I am in your service and I honor you, An Mórrígan.

Go raibh maith agat.

85.

An Mórrígan, hear my prayer. Great Queen, I honor you.

I ask for your protection, An Mórrígan.

May I remain safe from any dangers, both known and unknown.

May no attack against me come to fruition.

May the words of those that would spread lies about me turn to dust

And may the power of their intention against me fade.

May I be safeguarded so that I can do the work that you ask of me without distraction.

Hear me, An Mórrígan. I am faithful to you, Goddess.

May I be kept safe from any danger that would try to harm me or mine.

With your help, may I be aware of my surroundings

And not take my security for granted. May I have wisdom.

Thank you for your protection, Goddess.

With your help, may I be wise and aware in my daily life.

May I stay safe, in all things, as we work together.

I thank you for your protection and direction, An Mórrígan.

I honor you always, Great Queen.

Go raibh maith agat.

86.

An Mórrígan, you are known to protect those that work with you

And that are faithfully doing the work.

Hear my prayer, Great Queen. I ask for your help with a threat that has been made against me

Goddess, see the situation is threatening to cause me harm.

An Mórrígan, I ask that you defend me.

I ask that you trouble any intention again me, Great Queen,

And that you steal the motivations of my enemies that are held against me.

An Mórrígan, I am faithful to you. Grant me your aid, Great Queen.

Goddess of battle and sovereignty, I ask in your name,

I ask that you interfere with any plots against me.

With my greatest respect and sincere need, An Mórrígan,

I ask that any attacks against me be blocked.

May any attempts to injury me be weakened,

May any actions against me wane and fade from my existence.

I ask that my enemies that are acting against me be defeated, Goddess,

And that they be unable to do any harm to me or those belonging to me.

In your name, An Mórrígan, may I be given favor and victory in this situation

And above all else, may I be safe and kept from unnecessary danger.

Thank you for your protection from this calamity rising against me, Goddess.

Thank you, generous An Mórrígan, for your intervention. I honor you always.

Honor to you forever, An Mórrígan. Goddess fierce and powerful, I honor you.

Go raibh maith agat.

87.

Honor to you, An Mórrígan. Hear my prayer, Great Queen.

Receive my offerings and hear my prayers.

Goddess over warriors and warriorship, may I have wisdom as I face my battles.

May I be safe from bodily harm as I do the work you put before me.

May my protection be assured, An Mórrígan, and the peace of safety be upon me.

I will work to face the fears that try to overcome me.

I will work to stand confidently in my truth with respect for myself and others.

May I gather my resilience and resolve to stand beside those in need of justice

And to give aid during times of danger and crisis, as I am able.

May wisdom stay with me. May I not engage in battles beneath me

Or that would cause me undue harm.

I honor you and I thank you, Great Queen.

May I follow your guidance at all times.

May I remain safe as I work for you and with you, An Mórrígan.

I will take responsibility for my actions and I will not put myself recklessly in the path

Of situations that I am not prepared for. May I have wisdom as I do my work.

I am in your service with devotion, honor, loyalty, and love.

Go raibh maith agat.

88.

Hear my prayer, An Mórrígan. I honor you, Great Queen.

Goddess of sovereignty, you are known to defend those that are yours.

I ask for your aid and protection in a sincere time of need.

By your influence, An Mórrígan, may any threats against me become powerless.

May they lose their heat, and become like dead ashes long after a fire has burned out.

May they lose their strength, and become as frail as the dust on a moth's wings.

May they threat become soundless, voiceless, powerless, and have no impact on me.

May any threats against my security not reach me.

May I be safe in all things, Great Queen.

May my efforts to do the work you give me be secure from interference.

I honor you this day and all days, An Mórrígan.

And with my loyalty, I will do the work you ask of me

I will continue to show up daily for you, Goddess.

I thank you, Great Queen, for your protection on me and my home.

Thank you for safeguarding me and all that belongs to me.

Go raibh maith agat. Honor to you always, An Mórrígan.

89.

An Mórrígan, Goddess of sovereignty and battle, hear this prayer.

I honor you, Goddess renown for your power and skill with satire and sorcery.

Great Queen, I ask that you intervene on my behalf,

With a situation that is threatening to bring me harm.

So that I'm kept safe, I ask for your protection during this time.

An Mórrígan, I have explored all the ways to manage this issue on my own.

If there there is a way to reassess this problem

Which appears to be unsolvable to me, help me to see it.

I thank you for your guidance.

Hear my prayers, An Mórrígan. I am devoted to you, Great Queen.

I ask that you defend me as long as required, until this issue is resolved.

May my safety be assured, Goddess.

An Mórrígan, see me in my time of need.

Thank you for your guidance.

I will answer you in the time that you call for me.

I am here for you, Great Queen. I will answer when you call for me.

I am grateful for your help in this matter, Mórrígu.

Honor to you forever, Great Queen.

Go raibh maith agat.

90.

Hear my prayer, An Mórrígan, Goddess of sovereignty and battle. I honor you.

See me, Goddess, in my time of need.

An Mórrígan, you are known to always defend what is yours,

And I am yours, Great Queen. May safety stay with me always as we work together.

Protect me, An Mórrígan,

From any calamity that looms over me, whether known or unknown to me,

And may any threat not reach me.

An Mórrígan, may I be safeguarded against any danger.

May the source of any threat lose sight of me

And may it no longer remember my name.

May disaster not cross my path.

May time be on my side in times of concern. May I be delivered to safety,

And in that safety, may I be kept.

May security be present in my life, for myself and my loved ones. May I have peace,

And with that peace, I will focus on the worthy work you have given to me.

Honor to you forever, Great Queen. I thank you for aid, mighty Goddess.

Go raibh maith agat.

91.

I call to you, An Mórrígan, great Goddess of battle and bringer of victory.

I honor you. Hear me, Great Queen. I ask for your help, Mórrígu.

I come to you now with a petition for your help and intervention.

An Mórrígan, I ask for shelter during this time of danger and uncertainty

That has come to my door.

May my home be safe and well-guarded with protection upon all that live therein.

See me safely through my battles and after each day's work,

See me safely to my rest, Great Queen.

An Mórrígan, Goddess of battle and sovereignty,

Mighty daughter of Ernmas, sister of Macha and the Badb,

Hear my prayer and receive my offerings.

I honor you forever, An Mórrígan.

Go raibh maith agat.

92.

An Mórrígan, hear my prayer and receive my offerings.

I honor you with great respect.

As I walk this path into the unknown each day

I ask that my safety be ensured, Great Queen.

An Mórrígan, I ask for your protection in my daily life,

And that I be kept safe from any attempts to harm me.

If there are threats against me, Great Queen,

May I be kept safe from their attacks.

If there are actions made against me, may they fail.

May those that would come against me be gone,

Blown away like dry leaves crushed under my feet.

Great Queen, may I be kept safe.

If there is anyone that would wish me ill,

May they fade away from my personal life.

Great Queen, keep me safe from any dangers known or unknown.

May none be able to harm me, living or dead, human or not.

Thank you for seeing to my safety, An Mórrígan.

Go raibh maith agat.

93.

An Mórrígan, I call out to you. Hear this prayer, Great Queen.

I am your devotee, Goddess, and I am faithful to you.

I ask for your help, An Mórrígan.

I ask for your intervention, Goddess, to change this situation

That has emerged in my life and is threatening to do me harm.

An Mórrígan, I ask for your aid with this threat.

May the tides turn in my favor and bring me the upper hand.

Great Queen, I ask that this danger, this distraction to my work, be snuffed out.

Let my path and daily life settle back into stability and my security be assured.

Goddess deserving of honor and praise, An Mórrígan, I call out to you.

May I and all belonging to me be safeguarded during this time of uncertainty.

May this danger pass over me and fade into nothing without causing me harm.

Thank you, Great Queen, for your intervention on my behalf.

Give me the work you want from me and I will do it.

I honor you, An Mórrígan. I honor you now and I honor you always,

Go raibh maith agat.

## Prayers Asking for Wisdom, Guidance, and Insight

94.

An Mórrígan, Goddess that speaks prophecies and gives incitement through poetry,

I honor you. Hear my prayer, Great Queen.

Goddess that brings the strategies for great change that will unfold in this world,

May your changes bring about a return to sovereignty and rightness

And bring devastation to the powers of oppression.

May I have the wisdom to examine my beliefs and question my mindsets.

May I have wisdom to know how and when to take action

To stand for the causes of justice and support positive change.

I ask for your guidance, An Mórrígan.

May I be given insight into the ways I can hold space for justice

And know the ways I can best contribute.

May I have the courage to always support the voices that fight and stand

For dignity and sovereignty for all people.

May I have wisdom when I act and give my support.

I honor you, Great Queen. You have my loyalty and my devotion.

May I do the work that honors you.

Go raibh maith agat.

95.

An Mórrígan, I call to you, Goddess great and powerful.

May I have wisdom in the ways I conduct myself

and how to live my life with purpose and rightness.

May I have insights into what rightness means for my life.

May I have wisdom when dealing with people,

Both in the communities I am a part of,

And the personal connections that support me.

May I weigh my intentions against the judgments of wisdom.

With your guidance, Great Queen, may I begin to distinguish what is honorable,

So I have the opportunity to choose the honorable path.

I ask for your guidance and support as I seek to achieve

Honor and rightness in my daily life.

I ask these things in your name, An Mórrígan.

May I serve you and work with you honorably and with rightness.

I honor you forever, An Mórrígan.

Thank you for your wisdom and guidance.

Go raibh maith agat.

96.

An Mórrígan, hear my prayer. I honor you, Great Queen.

May a pathway of communication be open between us, Great Queen,

With a space within me available and receptive to you always

So that I can receive your guidance when you provide it.

May I hear clearly and may I listen.

I invite and I ask for a deeper communication

So that I may receive your guidance and instruction.

May I receive the wisdom you share with me

And apply it to my life and the work I do.

I will listen for your guidance, Great Queen.

May I be awakened to the ways you speak to me, and

I will do my best to be attentive and aware

So that I can listen with a conscious mind.

I honor you, An Mórrígan, with my devotion and respect.

Go raibh maith agat.

97.

An Mórrígan, Goddess present and watchful over the battlefield,

Hear my prayer. I honor you, Great Queen.

Thank you for your time and your investment in my life as we work together.

Thank you for the challenges I have had to face

And the opportunities to prove myself.

I am grateful that nothing has been brought to me

That I didn't have the strength to bear.

An Mórrígan, I ask that you look after me in the times that I struggle and

During those challenging times when I most need your guidance,

Whether or not I have the clarity to ask for it.

May I work through through those periods and gain insights

Into them whenever possible for my growth.

With your guidance, Great Queen, may I understand

How to thrive and do my work despite them.

I honor you, Goddess of battle poetry, sovereignty, and prophecy.

Honor to you forever, An Mórrígan. I am honored to be counted among your devotees

And part of your community. I am grateful to you and I will be loyal to you, always.

Go raibh maith agat.

98.

Honor to you, An Mórrígan. Great Queen, hear my prayer.

Sovereignty Goddess, you gave guidance and aid to the mighty Dagda,

And counseled him before battle.

Mighty strategist, I ask for your guidance with the battles that I face.

Goddess, may I have wisdom to proceed with rightness

And maintain security in my life.

May my growth be well supported by my actions.

May I gain insights into how to create the momentum needed

To move forward with my goals and my desires.

May I have the wisdom to understand the ways to best support myself.

An Mórrígan, Goddess of battle and sovereignty, I ask for your guidance

To know which battles are worthy of me and which battles are not.

May I act with bravery paired with wisdom and may my instincts

Be aligned with rightness. May wisdom be with me, Great Queen.

I honor you, An Mórrigan, and I thank you for your guidance.

Go raibh maith agat.

99.

An Mórrígan, hear my prayer. I honor you, mighty Goddess.

May I receive your guidance in the times when I need it. May I listen.

May I have your insights into the ways to give aid

To the issues I've been led to support

And how to battle for them, in the ways I am able.

Great Queen, I ask that you give me guidance through my battles,

So that I am effective with my efforts.

May my experiences contribute to my growth, and may my choices

Reflect the progress I have made. May I have wisdom.

May I keep my focus and resolve

As I put forth the effort as I do the work I've agreed to.

May I have the strength and the resources

To complete all tasks you have asked of me.

Honor to you, An Mórrígan.

My service and devotion are yours, Great Queen.

Go raibh maith agat.

100.

An Mórrígan, hear my prayer. Great Queen, I honor you.

Goddess associated with sovereignty, prophecy, and incitement,

I ask for your guidance in my life.

May I gain insight into the challenges I experience,

And may I be open to growth when I face them.

May I learn what I can from them, Great Queen,

And may I examine if I contributed, knowingly or not

To those difficult experiences. May I gain wisdom from them.

Great Queen, may I have insights into the potential within myself.

May I be objective when I consider which are my strongest attributes,

Which traits are most worthy of development,

And which are most in need of corrective action.

May I have the wisdom to identify the most beneficial skills

That could aid the causes you have led me to support.

I ask for your wisdom and guidance throughout my life, An Mórrígan,

To lead me to the ways to best serve you, Goddess.

Honor to you always, Great Queen.

Go raibh maith agat.

101.

An Mórrígan, Goddess with knowledge and the skill of prophecy,

Who keeps all things under her watchful eye, I honor you.

Hear my prayer, Great Queen.

Goddess, in the form of a crow, you came to the Donn Cuailnge

And gave him warning and guidance.

I ask, Great Queen, if there is an occasion I should be warned about,

Or if there is something in the distance coming for me,

May I hear your warning and guidance.

An Mórrígan, give me guidance in the times I am unaware and unprepared,

So that I have the time to prepare myself.

May I hear your guidance, Great Queen.

May I listen and may I understand.

Thank you, Great Queen. May you receive the offerings I bring you

With my undying respect and devotion, Goddess.

I honor you, always. Go raibh maith agat.

102.

An Mórrígan, hear my prayer. I honor you, Great Queen.

I ask for help to gain insight into the work you've given me

And how I can improve the ways I am contributing.

May I be open to the insights I receive

As I seek to understand the ways I can optimize my efforts

And maintain balance so that my mundane needs are met.

When I gain insights, may I consider how they best apply

To my life and my decisions.

May I understand those insights with clarity and objectivity.

May I record those insights faithfully for my future reference.

I ask this so I am more effective and successful

With the work I do for you, An Mórrígan.

I ask so that I can better understand and improve

My own usefulness to you, Great Queen.

I honor you always. Go raibh maith agat.

103.

Honor to you, An Mórrígan. Powerful and unfailing Goddess, I honor you.

Great Queen, hear my prayer and receive my offerings.

I ask for your help, An Mórrígan, so I have wisdom to skillfully balance

the mundane needs in my life, my relationships with loved ones,

And the investment of time needed for the work we do together.

I will stand by my promises to you and be faithful to them, An Mórrígan.

May I know how to manage myself and my time effectively

so that I am efficient and practical,

And so I have sufficient time to focus on both spiritual and mundane activities.

In order to better do the work you have for me,

May I be guided to where I need to focus my efforts,

Especially for my healing and growth.

May I have your support when the work becomes difficult.

I will remain aware in regards to my accountability.

May your support, wisdom, and insight be with me

As I walk my path in service and in agreement with you.

Honor to you, mighty An Mórrígan. My loyalty to you always.

Go raibh maith agat.

104.

An Mórrígan, hear my voice, mighty Goddess of sovereignty and battle.

I bring you offerings, prayers to honor you, and my respect.

I ask for your guidance, Great Queen, with addressing the issues I face in my life.

May my choices be conscious and my actions be consistent.

May I have the wisdom to understand that with change comes growth,

And with growth comes accountability,

And that accountability will bring work.

May accountability help me find the strength within myself.

May I have the opportunity to support the positive changes and growth in others.

May I have the wisdom to not fear the changes I need in my life.

May I have wisdom as I walk this path and do the good work.

Honor to you forever, Great Queen. Go raibh maith agat.

## Prayers Asking to Invoke Change

These prayers are written as invitations to the Mórrígan to create the changes needed in the life of the person saying the prayer. They ask her aid to invoke change: whatever is needed to course-correct, develop wisdom or growth, in order to heal, or to become more useful to her. If the Mórrígan chooses to do this, then be fully aware that a change may be drastic or surrounding something unexpected. It may not be a drastic change, of course, but I recommend personalizing the prayers to specify any boundaries or avoid offering anything that isn't desired.

In part, writing these prayers was a required exercise to work towards facing my fears and hesitation about change. While writing these prayers has been helpful to me, I cannot claim to have prayed them to her.

I am not saying that the Mórrígan necessarily requires an invitation to create needed changes in the lives of her devotees: she may choose to act regardless. These prayers are calling out to her saying that you are ready for whatever changes are needed: external changes needed as a catalyst, changes for well-being and growth, or changes needed to make space for her and the work to be done for her in your life. I believe prayers inviting change may be helpful if your current situation has become so stifled that escape is needed from it by any change necessary, or that you are ready to shift onto whatever path that will most aid your usefulness to the Mórrígan. Be aware that doing so might be inviting your life to be turned upside down if that's what is needed for your healing and growth.

105.

An Mórrígan, sorceress, satirist, strategist,

And the bringer of great change, I call to you.

Hear me, Goddess. I call out to you for aid, Great Queen.

I am in your service and I put my trust in your wisdom.

I ask that you bring me the catalyst that will shape me

To become my most useful and beneficial version of myself.

I desire to become more useful to you and to experience the growth

I need in my life. I ask that change come to my life.

I invite removal of anything that blocks my progress,

If there is something in my external life that you can remove

That would begin a catalyst of changes in my life.

Hear me, An Mórrígan. Hear me, Great Queen.

I call out to you to aid my change and to bring it about by your strategy.

Goddess that I love and I am dedicated to, An Mórrígan, hear my prayer.

I am willing to face any change.

I am willing to embrace the unknown.

I am willing to face any cost,

If you stand by me and help me rebuild.

I honor you, An Mórrígan.

I honor you now, Great Queen, and I honor you always.

Shape my path and environment that will create the needed changes in me.

I am ready. Go raibh maith agat.

106.

An Mórrígan, see me. An Mórrígan, hear me.

Goddess of battle and sovereignty, I am yours.

Hear my petition, Great Queen.

I have total trust in your foresight, strategy, and guidance.

I invite the changes needed in my life

That allow me to deepen my relationship with you

And that leads me to becoming my most effective and useful self.

In whatever shape the change comes in

As long as there is no harm.

I invite what change in life would most benefit me,

I am ready, Great Queen.

Move what needs to be moved in my life.

Force me to become stronger and more able

To do the work you have for me.

Wherever change is needed in my life,

I pray that need be met by your hand,

So that I can grow and heal in my life.

Thank you for helping me to bring about these changes, An Mórrígan.

I will remain faithfully in your service, and to what I have promised you,

Throughout these times of this change being brought to me.

Go raibh maith agat.

107.

An Mórrígan, hear my voice.

Goddess of incitement and battle, I honor you.

I invite the change needed for my growth and survival,

No matter how difficult,

No matter the cost,

No matter what my path becomes, as long as it leads to obtaining

A deepened relationship and more successful work with you.

An Mórrígan, I am ready to embrace any changes needed with your guidance.

You have my trust. You have my devotion and my service.

An Mórrígan, I want to be free from any blocks that are causing a distance

Between us. Help me, Great Queen, by removing those blocks or by causing the changes

That will become the catalyst for their removal.

I am ready to let go of what I need to.

With my trust and my devotion,

I invite any changes in my external life that will support my growth,

And I will continue to work on bringing about my needed changes within.

An Mórrígan, I am willing to be dismantled and rebuilt.

I am willing to face a battlefield of change.

I am willing for my life to turn upside down, if that is what is needed

To continue my journey with you.

An Mórrígan, hear my voice and this prayer, An Mórrígan.

I honor you and will continue to do so my whole life, Great Queen. Go raibh maith agat.

108.

Honor to you, An Mórrígan, whose delight is in mustered hosts.

Hear my prayer, Great Queen, and receive my offerings.

Goddess of sovereignty and battle, I give you my gratitude

For the growth, healing, and the positive changes I've experienced in my life.

Thank you for the gaining of sovereignty over my life.

Thank you for your guidance and your aid in the times that I have needed it.

Thank you for the work you have given me.

I would like to move further in our relationship.

Whatever changes are needed in my external life

For me to grow towards you,

Let those changes come.

Understanding that I may not realize what is needed

To go to the next level in our relationship,

I invite you, Great Queen, to make room in my life as needed,

And to invoke what external changes would best support my growth.

Deliver them in the ways you feel are most appropriate

For what I can handle in my current state, An Mórrígan.

May those changes in my life come, Goddess of sovereignty.

I trust in your judgment with what I can achieve and what I can manage.

I ask for your guidance with how to proceed when the changes come.

I honor you forever, Great Queen. Go raibh maith agat.

## Prayers Asking for Strength

109.

An Mórrígan, Goddess I am devoted to you with my whole self.

Goddess of sovereignty and battle, I honor you.

May I have the strength to work steadily and consistently,

As much as I am possibly able to.

With your guidance and support, Great Queen,

May I continue to find the resolve I need

To stay faithful to the commitments I've promised you, Great Queen.

May I maintain the self care I need,

So that I do not become burdened or overwhelmed.

So that I can heal, to support my growth, and increase my wisdom and strength,

May I continue my shadow work, process the traumas within,

And dismantle all the oppressive indoctrination I was raised into.

May I access the untapped strength within myself,

So I remain capable of carrying on and doing my work.

May I reach deep within myself for strength, clarity, and resolve.

I am here whenever you call me. I honor you this day and all days, An Mórrígan.

I give you loyalty for all time, Great Queen, with respect and constancy.

Hear my words given to you, An Mórrígan.

Go raibh maith agat.

110.

Honor to you, An Mórrígan. Great Queen, hear my prayer.

As I face one day after another, and do the work I've been given,

Guide me forwards, Great Queen.

I will rise and do the work daily,

Day after day, to the best of my ability.

May I have the strength and persistence needed

In order to find triumph in my battles.

May I have clarity and focus on the tasks at hand.

May I give roots to my intent, reaching deep within and holding on.

May I be diligent in my studies and continue on my path towards healing.

May I stay aware of my actions and strive for rightness.

I honor you, mighty and eternal one,

Shape-shifting Goddess, An Mórrígan.

I honor you, Great Queen.

Go raibh maith agat.

111.

An Mórrígan, Goddess of sovereignty and battle,

Hear my prayer, Great Queen.

May I walk this path through my life, doing the work you have for me,

And may I become more capable of the actions presented before me

As I become stronger and wiser with my choices.

May I preserve my strength for what is needed,

And may I act with dutiful honor

To complete what I have promised to you, Great Queen.

I ask for your guidance through all needed changes in my life.

May I be successful in my efforts, and may they be useful to you.

An Mórrígan, with your guidance and for your purpose,

I will do the work you bring me to do. May it honor you.

Great Queen, I honor you. Go raibh maith agat.

112.

An Mórrígan, Goddess to whom I am devoted, hear my prayer.

I honor you, Great Queen.

Bringer of battle that leads to sovereignty and change,

You have called me to face my battles within.

Give me your blessing as I rise to face this difficult day.

May I have the strength to be fully present for this battle

And through all my battles I face within.

May I find my strength and renew it

In the times of solitude and peace.

May my strength be sufficient to do my work,

And may my efforts be aligned to rightness.

Watch over my efforts, Great Queen, and may they be worthy.

I call to you, mighty Goddess,

With the resolve to move forward on this path.

As I work to build up my own strength, An Mórrígan,

Move what needs to be altered in my life for my growth

And grant me the guidance to the become the most productive,

Successful, and effective version of myself.

My gratitude to you always, Great Queen.

Go raibh maith agat.

113.

Honor to you, An Mórrígan. Goddess of sovereignty and battle,

Guardian of sovereignty, and the sacred battle for it,

I ask for your time, Great Queen, and to hear this prayer.

The recent days have been difficult. They seemed to have blended together

Into one long walk through the wilderness. I will continue on, An Mórrígan.

May I have strength as I battle through this day

And see the end of it with no harm upon me.

Thank you for the safety provided to me.

May I battle through it honorably, An Mórrígan.

May I have the strength to do what I need to.

May I become stronger as I work for you and with you, An Mórrígan.

I ask you to lend me some strength if my own is fading,

So that in all things that come, I can be ready to face them.

May I continue on this path with devotion, diligence, and love.

May I continue on this path holding space for my own sovereignty

And space for the sovereignty of others. May I hold space for justice.

May I become the most honorable version of myself.

Honor to you, mighty An Mórrígan. My gratitude to you.

Go raibh maith agat.

114.

An Mórrígan, Goddess that brings great change

Though battle and strategy, hear my prayer.

I honor you, Great Queen.

I come to you at a time when my strength is spent.

On this challenging day, my strength isn't what I want it to be.

My desire is not waning. My commitments to you will stand.

An Mórrígan, may I build my strength as time goes by.

May I find my grounding in the face of overwhelm,

And may I be diligent with my self care.

I will rest. May I recover and be renewed.

So I can become stronger than I was before,

I will work to change in the ways I need to.

So that I can retain my strength and become stronger still,

I will be diligent in maintaining my boundaries

And be honest with what is and what isn't necessary.

May I be diligent in my actions to honor myself

And to honor you, An Mórrígan.

So that I can live my life with rightness

And realize my own value,

I will work to build my strength

To embrace what tomorrow will bring.

I honor you always, An Mórrígan. Go raibh maith agat.

115.

Honor to you, An Mórrígan.

May I be strengthened, Great Queen,

In the timing and measure that I can handle successfully,

So that I can thrive and be more useful to you.

May I strive onward, keeping to my boundaries and self-care.

In my time, may I have the strength to stand firm, from a power deep within me,

Standing firm against any battles that would seek to diminish me.

May my life be lived fully and without fear. May my strength resound within me.

May my courage be unflinching, once I have found it,

And my strength be unfailing, once I have built it.

In your name, An Mórrígan. I honor you now and always.

Go raibh maith agat.

116.

I honor you, An Mórrígan, Goddess of battle, incitement, and strategy.

You are powerful and unmatched, shape-shifting Goddess.

Satirist, you turned Ódras into a stream with your fierce chanting.

Sorceress, you pulled out the kidneys of valor from the king

That led the enemies of your people.

I honor you, An Mórrígan, mighty Goddess.

As the washer at the ford, washing the bloody weapons and entrails,

You washed the bloody gear and foretold the inevitable.

Help me face the truth, and the inevitable in my life, with strength.

In your name, An Mórrígan, may I have the strength needed

To maintain honor and rightness in my daily actions.

May my actions speak to justice and my actions speak to truth.

May I face my reality with strength, compassion, wisdom, and joy.

May I make choices with accountability and self-sovereignty.

With wisdom, may I maintain my self-care, guard my boundaries,

And preserve my strength, both for the battles I face

And the work you require of me.

May I stay consistent with caring for myself throughout my journey.

I honor you, Great Queen. I will continue to honor you

Till the long journey of my life ends.

Go raibh maith agat.

117.

An Mórrígan, with my greatest respect and devotion,

I call out to you. Hear my prayer, Great Queen.

Goddess of incitement, battle, warriorship, sovereignty, and prophecy,

I honor you always. May my efforts for you remain sincere throughout my life.

May I have the strength to carry on with the tasks given to me

And the tasks I have promised and offered to you.

May I face the challenges in my life,

With a mind that is focused and receptive

And a heart capable of both bravery and peace.

May I have the strength to face the battles that wait for me -

Both the battles that exist within me

And the battles for justice that exist in the world.

Goddess, you make the way for sovereignty,

Justice, and the bringing about of great and needed changes.

May I have the strength to stand beside others

In the name of sovereignty and justice

And to hold space for stories and voices that are unheard

Due to the strongholds of oppression.

May I have the strength to work bravely for you, An Mórrígan,

And to do the work in your name.

Honor to you, Great Queen. Honor to you forever. Go raibh maith agat.

118.

An Mórrígan, hear my prayer. Great Queen, I honor you.

May the work of my hands remain inspired by the passion of my intent.

May I answer your call to battle, to face my battles within

And hold space for justice in the time given to me. May I build my strength

And manage only what I can handle safely.

May I gain an understanding of when to work and when to rest.

May I rest. May I care for my needs and all belonging to me.

May I have the strength to begin anew when needed.

With a willingness to learn and adapt,

May I embrace the changes that lay before me

And not resist them as I have in the past.

May I have the strength to face the changes when they come.

I am devoted to you, An Mórrígan,

This work I do is committed to you.

With your guidance, I will make the space in my life

Needed for your work.

With courage and consistency, Great Queen,

May I recognize the moments when I can support positive change.

Whenever I face injustice, with wisdom, may I hold space for myself and others.

I honor you, Great Queen. May I live and work as closely aligned

With rightness as I am capable of.

Praise and honor to you, An Mórrígan. Go raibh maith agat.

## Prayers for aid in Battle and Battle-themed Prayers

119.

Hear my prayer, An Mórrígan, Goddess of sovereignty.

Goddess who awakens us to rise to our battles

And incites the warriorship within us, I honor you.

Goddess that washes bloody spoils at the ford,

Watch over my battles through my life

And my journey until I reach its end.

Watch over my growth on this path that I walk,

And grant me your guidance, Great Queen.

An Mór Ríoghain, I call out to you in my devotion.

You have my fealty and my unflinching loyalty, An Mórrígan.

An Mór Ríoghain, battle crow,

Goddess of battle and sovereignty,

Goddess terrible in power and fury,

Goddess triumphant in battle.

Goddess who brings victory,

An Mór Ríoghain, I honor you.

May I build my strength as I walk this path and carry onward with my tasks.

May my strength be renewed whenever needed, Great Queen.

May I face the battles that come to my path honorably throughout my life.

Go raibh maith agat.

120.

An Mórrígan, shape-shifting Goddess and wielder of magic,

Hear my prayer. Great Queen, I honor you.

Giver of battle, poetry, and incitement,

I call out to you asking for guidance with the battle I face.

May I possess clarity in my intent. May I act with wisdom.

I come to you with offerings, An Mórrígan.

Sorceress, prophetess, I give you due honor and respect.

During my times of study and devotion, may my focus be strengthened.

Incite me for the battle within, An Mórrígan. May I rise to face it.

Send me to a worthy cause to fight for.

Send me with the purpose for my battle in this world.

May I train with vigilance, however that looks for me,

And may I be faithful to it.

May I remember to tend to my self-care and rest

To be at my best for the work you have for me.

I honor you, An Mórrígan. Thank you for your time and your presence, Great Queen.

Go raibh maith agat.

121.

Hear my prayer, An Mórrígan. Sovereignty Goddess of Ireland, I honor you.

Goddess of battle-incitement, battle poetry, and prophecy,

Shape-shifting Goddess, I honor you, Great Queen.

You have defended your people with sorcery, strategy, and guile.

You have taken the strength of your people's enemies with fistfuls of blood.

You pursue what was watched and are able to kill.

I honor you and I am here for you, Goddess. Hear my prayer.

Aid me in my battle and towards my victory.

In your name, An Mórrígan, may I be incited to rise up

And awake to meet my battle within.

For my growth and my self-sovereignty, I will battle.

I honor you Great Queen. May I rise when I need to rise.

May I awake and rise up. May I battle when I need to battle.

May victory be laid on my path with your aid.

Goddess over warriors and sacred warriorship,

Great Queen, I honor you.

Go raibh maith agat.

122.

An Mórrígan, Great Queen present on the battlefield,

You incite battle and bring change.

You give rise to the warrior within.

Guide me to my inner battles

That I've attempted to ignore and push aside.

See me safely through them, Goddess.

Lead me to the causes of my inner battles and may I face them.

May I remember that I don't need to hide the scars of my survival.

May I achieve victory over my inner battles.

In your name, An Mórrígan, may I obtain and exist with self-sovereignty in my life,

And may I battle to defend it when necessary.

May I have the strength, courage, and wisdom I need

To battle for the worthy causes you lead me to,

Especially the cause of my own well-being and growth.

Honor to you forever, Great Queen.

Go raibh maith agat.

123.

An Mórrígan, giver of triumph,

I call to you as I stand before the battle that waits for me.

May I find victory at the end of it.

May I rise to meet the challenges I will face.

May good fortune be with me. May you be with me, Great Queen.

I ask that you watch me, Goddess. Incite me when I need it.

Guide me if ever I lose my way.

Remind me, in your way, if am neglecting my work

So that I have the opportunity to find my footing

And begin my work again.

May I prepare to face whatever battles lay before me and are within me.

As I study, train, work, and reflect,

May I have clarity.

I honor you, shape-shifting Goddess, with my whole heart.

I honor you with loyalty and respect.

I honor you with devotion.

May my battles be won with rightness and resolve.

May my efforts honor you, An Mórrígan.

Go raibh maith agat.

124.

Honor to you, An Mórrígan, shape-shifting Goddess that appeared

As a she-wolf, an eel, a hornless red heifer leading a stampede of cattle,

And as a crow sitting on a standing stone,

giving guidance and incitement to the Donn Cuailnge.

I honor you, shape-shifting Goddess,

You who incite the battle and bring change,

You who see the valor of warriors on the battlefield

And those born in battle.

You who proclaim the victory and the defeat of the battle,

Goddess, see me in my battles.

May I face them with courage and wisdom

And may my actions honor you, An Mórrígan.

Guide me to the ways I can be useful to you, Great Queen.

Show me the work you expect of me and my part, however great or small.

I honor you, An Mórrígan, with my respect, loyalty, devotion, and love.

Honor to you forever, Great Queen.

Go raibh maith agat

125.

Honor to you, An Mórrígan.

Hear my voice and receive my offerings, Great Queen.

You are very welcome here, Goddess.

An Mórrígan, with a watchful eye over the battlefield,

You bring victory and demand sovereignty.

Goddess of battle that gives incitement for the battle,

I ask that you bring forth the inner battles needed for my growth,

And the battles I must face to obtain my sovereignty.

May I gather wisdom from these experiences

And may my determination be unfaltering.

May I stay focused on the daily actions that maintain my well-being.

During the times of great challenges,

May I battle through any blocks that may be hindering my success.

May I continue on my path with courage and devotion.

My gratitude to you forever, Great Queen. I honor you, Goddess.

Go raibh maith agat.

126.

Hear my voice, An Mór Ríoghain.

Goddess working through satire, sorcery, and poetry,

Working by prophecy and shape-shifting,

Great Queen inciting warriors and leaders to rise,

Goddess giving victory and triumph in battle,

An Mór Ríoghain, I honor you.

Hear my prayer, mighty Goddess of battle,

These words I speak to you, with my respect,

And I thank you for hearing them.

May I work through my battles and see my truth.

May I gain my sovereignty over myself and defend it.

May I take back control of my own life,

And live a better life because of it.

May I be awakened to my battle. May I rise and take hold of my challenges.

I ask for your guidance and support with these things,

An Mór Ríoghain, Goddess of battle and sovereignty, I honor you.

Go raibh maith agat.

127.

An Mórrígan, sovereignty Goddess of Ireland,

Goddess with the power to give and remove kingship

For the good of the people and the guardianship of the land,

I honor you with respect and devotion.

As I battle through my self-doubt in order to do my work,

May I hold space for the voices of those that are excluded,

That are battling for equal dignity and rights,

And may I support their efforts and stand beside them.

May I never lose sight of the sacred purpose of that work.

May my efforts be aligned with rightness as I work to support positive change.

May I defend the individual sovereignty of all people,

As well as for myself.

May I hold space for others in every way that I am able.

May I have the courage to stand for truth in the face of injustice.

With wisdom, may I allow my voice to be heard.

An Mórrígan, Goddess of sovereignty, I honor you.

Go raibh maith agat.

128.

Honor to you, An Mórrígan, Goddess that brings incitement and prophecy.

Mighty Goddess, I call to you with respect.

May I remain persistent with my efforts

As I battle through my struggles with inner conflict.

With your guidance, may I be successful in my battles for clarity and peace.

An Mórrígan, may I find the focus I need to complete my work

Despite the challenges I face.

May I become established in my routines for productiveness

And find the rhythm and momentum that supports my efforts.

May I be successful with the work that you require of me, Goddess.

May I support my well-being with self-care and rest.

May I rise daily to do my work and battle through

My challenges when they come with patience, courage, and wisdom.

I honor you, Great Queen. I honor you forever.

Go raibh maith agat.

129.

An Mórrígan, powerful sorceress and satirist,

Prophetess, and Goddess of sovereignty, I honor you.

Goddess present and watchful over the battlefield, hear my prayer.

May I fight for for the causes you have led me to, Great Queen,

In the ways I am able. May I hold space for positive change

And stand beside those that tirelessly fight for it.

An Mórrígan, may there be justice for the oppressed.

May space be given to the voices unheard

And the cruelties of oppressors be exposed.

I will listen to the stories of those fighting for equal dignity and justice.

May I support those voices, Great Queen.

May any abuse done by corrupt people in authority be revealed to the world,

And may they be forced to face justice at their own cost.

An Mórrígan, may justice be an inescapable horror to false kings

And the powers of oppression be dismantled.

May unfit rulers fall for the good of the people.

May there be justice, so there can be rightness and peace.

May this world return to rightness, and health return to the land.

Honor to you, An Mórrígan. May I battle for the causes of rightness

In every way I am able. May I hold space for justice.

Go raibh maith agat.

130.

An Mórrígan, you incite the warriors to rise in valor.

May I receive incitement from you, Great Queen,

When those times come in my life.

Guide me on how to strengthen my resolve,

And be emboldened and to stand with others for justice, in the ways I am able.

May I learn to achieve a calm focus that is present and aware.

May I rise to do the work you require of me

And be available to you, whenever you call.

I honor you, mighty Goddess, Great Queen,

Thank you for hearing my prayer.

Thank you for receiving my offerings.

I honor you, Great Queen. I honor you always.

Go raibh maith agat.

131.

Hear my prayer, An Mórrígan. Goddess of battle and sovereignty, I honor you.

May I bring my willingness to train and work

And look deep within myself to find my mettle.

When I face my battles, may I find my strength within myself.

When I face my battles, may I honor you.

May my efforts be a worthy offering that honors you, An Mórrígan.

As I work to support causes of justice and sovereignty,

May my intentions be aligned with rightness.

An Mórrígan, may I awake to the battles I must undertake,

Without yielding. May my battles be grounded in wisdom.

Great Queen, mighty Goddess, I honor you.

Go raibh maith agat.

132.

Great Queen, hear my prayer. I honor you.

May I have your support and guidance, An Mórrígan,

As I work to dismantle any limiting mindsets

And self-destructive patterns in my life.

May the traumatic experiences in my past

Not rob me of my courage.

Rather, may they inspire me to fight harder

And to value myself as a survivor.

I ask for your help, Goddess, as I work steadily

To meet my inner battles and challenges.

May I be safe as I address them and not lose my way.

May I be safeguarded in my battles and have victory.

I honor you, An Mórrígan. I value your guidance

And I am grateful for your protection and aid.

Go raibh maith agat.

133.

An Mórrígan, sovereignty Goddess of Ireland,

Battle-crow present on the battlefield,

Great Queen whose pleasure is in mustered hosts,

Hear my prayer, Great Queen.  I honor you.

However you have use for me, An Mórrígan,

May I give my best efforts. May I rise and awake

To the battles you lead me to.

Guide me through my battles, An Mórrígan.

What skills I possesses, or the potential skills within me,

May I develop them to be useful to you

And the work you have for me,

May I receive your guidance, Great Queen.

Go raibh maith agat.

134.

An Mórrígan, hear my prayer. I honor you, Goddess.

Great Queen I ask for your guidance that I understand

What battle means to me in my life,

The best ways for to meet the battles I will face,

And what skills I can bring to support your great work.

May I know the ways to effectively contribute with what I have to offer.

May I have your guidance so I understand how to best offer my support.

An Mórrígan, I ask that you guide me to the battles that are meant for me

And to the work you have for me.

May I face them with courage and clarity.

Give me the strength and resources needed to complete my tasks.

May I do them with rightness in my heart

And gratitude for the opportunity.

I honor you, An Mórrígan. My loyalty to you always.

Go raibh maith agat.

135.

An Mórrígan, hear my prayer. Great Queen, I honor you.

Goddess that is renown for satire and sorcery, I give you my respect.

May I continue making progress in the ways that I am able.

Great Queen, may I be aided by you as I face my battles.

Show me how my skills can be applied on my personal battlefield,

For any battles that will come, whether external or within.

May your guidance stay with me on my path, Great Queen,

And help me with my chosen craft and the skills I'm building.

Goddess, may I act with courage when courage in battle is needed.

May I contemplate what battle means to me,

With the understanding that battle in some form will be part of my path.

In my battles may I stand with rightness and honor.

When you call for me to stand in battle, may I be available to you,

And have the opportunity to fight for the causes important to me.

May I witness their triumphs in my lifetime.

May my efforts honor you, Great Queen, and may they be known to you.

I honor you, An Mórrígan, Goddess of sovereignty.

You have my gratitude forever, Great Queen.

Go raibh maith agat.

136.

Hear my voice, An Mórrígan, Goddess of sovereignty and magic,

Of battle and cattle raids, and of warriorship and fate.

Goddess that brought showers of sorcery against the enemies of her people,

I honor you. May I discover my strength and victory in my battles.

May I prove myself worthy of my battles by engaging in them honorably

And by embracing my challenges with respect for myself.

When the times comes to stand for myself and my beliefs,

May I have wisdom and clarity. May I honor you, Mórrígu.

May I answer you, Great Queen, when you call for me.

May the work you give me prepare me for my battles.

I honor you forever, Great Queen.

Go raibh maith agat.

137.

An Mórrígan, hear my prayer.

May I prove to be worthy of my battles by the courage I greet them with.

May the fight within me be engaged and unyielding.

An Mórrígan, grant me the strength to continue onward

Through my battles and challenges in my life that are mine alone,

And may I remember that I am not alone. You are with me, Great Queen.

When my battles are over, may I rest and be renewed, and ready to stand again once more.

May your guidance be on my training and growth throughout the rest of my life.

Mórrígu, I commit myself to the path of my own well-being.

Where my growth is needed in my life, may it come.

Where changes in my life will help me gain victory in my battles

And sovereignty over my life, may those changes come.

Under the care of your guidance, as we work together,

May I prevail. May I reclaim sovereignty over myself.

I honor you forever, Great Queen.

Go raibh maith agat.

138.

Battle-crow, giver of battle-poetry,

You incite the battle and the warriors that fight it.

You have given me purpose in my work

And have guided me to the battles I must face.

May I have the resources and strength,

To take action whenever you call for it.

I will set time aside each day, to be available to you.

May I hear you clearly and understand your guidance.

And may I listen to your direction when you provide it.

May my responses and my actions,

Be paired with wisdom, temperance, and respect.

May I carry on honorably

With the tasks you have given to me.

Lend me strength, Great Queen, if needed,

During the times that I am actively doing the work

And it becomes overwhelming. May I have clarity.

I will give you the respect and dedication you expect.

I honor you always, An Mórrígan.

Go raibh maith agat.

139.

An Mórrígan, hear my voice. Honor to you, powerful Goddess.

I am grateful you have set me on a path of self-sovereignty.

It is a path that will not accept subjugation

Or a denial of my rights. I will not relinquish the power within myself.

It is a path that fights for right action and justice.

Great Queen, embolden me to stand guard and defend myself

And others I am able. May I fight well for the causes you have led me to.

I ask you for your guidance in my training and preparation.

I ask that you aid me in the battles I will face

And your direction as I walk this path.

May I study your lore with a mind that's open to learning.

May I draw on the lessons from my experiences

And implement them into my life where appropriate.

May my thoughts be clear and my mind understanding.

May I be guided in the ways to build strength, focus, and persistence,

To aid me in any battle that may be coming.

May I be guided by you as I reclaim my sovereign self,

As I claim sacred sovereignty of my own person,

As I regain agency and ownership over my own life.

I ask for your guidance and for strength as I fight my battles,

And do the work I need to for you and for both of us, Great Queen.

Honor to you forever, An Mórrígan. Go raibh maith agat.

140.

Mórrígu, I honor you. Hear my prayers, Great Queen.

An Mór Ríoghain, ancient Goddess from Ireland,

Goddess of sacred sovereignty, foreseeing and master strategist,

Whose pleasure is in mustered hosts, I honor you.

May victory come to me and my protection be assured.

Incite me for the battles that my path will lead me to,

May my inner battles cause me to understand the support I need

And may I take the steps needed to obtain that support.

Bring me to my battle in the timing that is most advantageous.

Give me the wisdom to only engage in battles worthy of me.

Make me prepared and battle-ready, and when I am ready,

Send me into the fray, knowing you will be with me, guiding me.

Whatever battles I must face in this lifetime, be with me Great Queen.

May I face the battles given to me with unfailing focus, with power of will, and with honor,

All to the best of my ability. May I have the time and resolve to grow, Great Queen.

May I be bold and steady, and may I be victorious in life.

And when the time for it has come, may I be victorious in death.

I am in your service, Mórrígu. Hear me, Great Queen. See me.

My loyalty to you always, Great Queen.

Go raibh maith agat.

141.

Goddess of battle and sovereignty, An Mórrígan, I call to you with respect.

Goddess that sees the deaths on the battlefield, I honor you.

Goddess that incites before the battle and ensures victory for her people,

I honor you, An Mórrígan. Honor to you always.

Goddess of sorcery and incitement,

May your guidance be with me and guide me in my battles.

I ask for your incitement in the times that I need it, An Mórrígan.

Goddess I am devoted to,

Guide me to the knowledge I need,

Guide me to my victorious path,

And guide me through my training.

Ensure my victory in the battles before me, Great Queen.

May I have the tools and resource available that I need

To be successful at work you've given and will give me.

I ask that your guidance stay with me in all times that I need it.

I honor you forever, An Mórrígan.

Go raibh maith agat.

142.

Honor to you, An Mórrígan, Goddess of battle and sovereignty.

Goddess of warriorship and battle,

Of sovereignty and defense of the land and its people, I honor you.

You defended your people with battle-magic,

By giving magical injury to the enemy king by taking his kidneys of valor,

By showering blood and fire upon the enemy,

And fog and rains to hinder them.

Satirist that gave incitement to kings, I honor you.

Goddess that speaks prophecies, I honor you.

May justice be brought to this world where it is needed, Great Queen.

An Mórrígan, I honor you, Goddess.

Honor to you always, Great Queen.

Go raibh maith agat.

143.

Praise and honor to you, An Mórrígan, Goddess of battle.

Hear my prayer, Great Queen.

You see the battle before it begins,

Goddess of prophecy, nothing in the battle is hidden from you.

You know the champions and your warriors on the battlefield.

You reveal strengths and challenge weaknesses.

You have incited the battle and tested their valor.

An Mórrígan, I ask for your guidance in my times of battle.

I ask for your protection, if ever I should need it.

I ask that in my time, when my challenges come,

And my battles, that I rise to meet them.

Great Queen, I honor you.

Praise and honor to you, An Mórrígan.

Go raibh maith agat.

144.

An Mórrígan, hear my prayer, Great Queen.

I ask for your guidance, Goddess of sovereignty.

As I do the work to gain sovereignty in my life,

May I have the wisdom to know which battles

Are worthy of action and which are not.

May it honor you, An Mórrígan, when I face the battles in my life that are worthy of action.

May it honor you, An Mórrígan, when I walk away from the battles that need to be left behind.

I ask for your guidance, Great Queen, to recognize the difference.

May I honor the worthy battles in my life, and you, An Mórrígan, by taking action.

Thank you for your guidance and the work you've given me, An Mórrígan.

I honor you, Goddess of sovereignty.

Go raibh maith agat.

145.

An Mórrígan, hear this prayer that I offer you.

Yours is the battlefield and the warriors' battle-cry.

Yours is the beating of war drums

And a crow flying above the mustered hosts.

Yours is the triumph and terror of the battle.

Yours is sovereignty at any cost.

Yours is the slaying of the enemies of your people.

Yours were fistfuls of blood, giving magical injury to the enemy king.

May I honor each promise I have ever made to you.

Honor to the Goddess that leads and guides her own to reclaim their self-sovereignty

And battle, the worthy battles you lead them to, with honor.

Honor to the Goddess that gives incitement to her people.

An Mórrígan,  I honor you, mighty Goddess of sovereignty.

Go raibh maith agat.

## Prayers Against Oppression and for Sovereignty

146.

An Mórrígan, hear my prayer. I honor you, Great Queen.

Goddess that gives prophecy and incitement,

May the words of your prophecies resound in the present

And your incitement spur the battles for sovereignty.

May your crows pierce the quiet with their voices, the harbingers of change,

The voices of the people that work with you to hold space for justice,

May their voices shatter any walls against them

And may your community rise up in support.

Bringer of change, mighty Goddess, An Mórrígan,

May the earth have its healing and be defended

And may oppression be choked at its source.

Honor to you, An Mórrígan, Goddess of sovereignty.

Go raibh maith agat.

147.

An Mór Ríoghain, Goddess of battle and incitement.

Hear my prayer. I honor you.

Powerful are the words you speak,

Satirist with words of poetry and magic,

Prophetess with words of foretelling and undoing.

Goddess with words of incitement, you give empowerment and strength.

Strategist, may your plans unfold a mighty undoing

Upon all that needs to be undone in this world.

May the path for justice be open. May false rulers fall and worthy rulership rise.

May tyranny be exposed, for the survival of a better world.

An Mór Ríoghain, Goddess the brings change,

May the positive changes needed in this world come.

An Mór Ríoghain, nothing is beyond your sight or your power,

Go raibh maith agat.

148.

An Mórrígan, hear my prayer.

I honor you, Irish Goddess of sovereignty and battle.

Goddess that leads her own

To the battle well fought and victorious,

And through the battles that follow.

May I hear your guidance and follow your leadership.

I honor you, An Mórrígan, Goddess undefeated.

Your leadership strengthens your followers

And guides their needed changes and growth.

You empower your own to follow you into battle,

With the power of self-sovereignty,

To support the causes of justice

And needed changes in the world.

Honor to you, An Mórrígan, the wielder of great change.

Honor to you, Great Queen.

May your changes spread throughout this world,

For the healing of it.

Sorceress, prophetess, satirist, shape-shifting Goddess,

An Mórrígan I honor you.

Go raibh maith agat.

149.

Hear my prayer, An Mórrígan,

I honor you, Great Queen.

Irish goddess of battle and sovereignty,

Sacred Sovereignty, Sacred Prophecy,

Sacred Justice, Sacred terror, Sacred strategy,

Sacred queen of the battle and the battlefield.

May your crows spread across this world.

May false leaders fall, for the good of the people,

May false leaders fall, may their causes for oppression be defeated,

In whatever way you see fit, Great Queen.

Go raibh maith agat.

150.

An Mórrígan, hear my voice. Honor to you, Great Queen.

May there be justice against all oppression.

May self-sovereignty be defended for all people.

May the truth of oppressive forces and their actions be revealed.

May accountability be required and may it bring change.

May the changes come that bring healing.

May I understand what being honorable means as I seek it.

May I accept my accountability,

And see my own truths within, with honesty.

With courage and the desire for growth,

May I have the willingness to face my battles

And work on the changes needed in me.

May my accountability bring me focus.

May I take any actions needed and keep the intention

Of living an honorable life with rightness.

May I hold space for the changes that are coming.

Honor forever to you, Great Queen,

May the oppressed be given justice,

May corrupt leadership fail and fall.

Go raibh maith agat.

151.

An Mórrígan hear my prayer. I honor you, Great Queen.

You whose name was given in the Táin Bó Regamna

As, "Keen edged, small lipped, plain cloaked, hair,

Sharp shouting, fierceness, a phantom."

You are sharp shouting fierceness.

You are the invoking of power and prophecy.

You are the strategy that brings about great change

For the guardianship and healing of the land.

You are the undoing of oppressive powers

By leading people to gain their self-sovereignty,

And by your people defending the self-sovereignty of others

And holding space for the healing of justice and accountability.

Great Queen, may your plans unfold upon the face of this world without ceasing.

May your will bring about the great changes to come

And may none be able to stop it.

I honor you this day and I will honor you tomorrow.

I will honor you tomorrow and the days after that as well.

I will honor you for the rest of my days. May I be long lived.

I offer this prayer to you, An Mórrígan, with respect and devotion.

I work for your and with you, in your name, and to honor you.

Go raibh maith agat.

152.

Hear my prayer, Great Queen. I honor you, An Mórrígan.

Great Queen, you are powerful and mighty.

Fierce and devastating to the enemies of your people,

Great Queen, you are the terror on the battlefield

To those that are against your own.

Goddess that watches and leads into battle,

Watch over me as I face my personal battles.

Goddess that guides her own, shows them where their battles are,

And brings them to the path that leads to victory in their battles,

May I be prepared and led to the battles I must face in my lifetime.

I honor you, An Mórrígan.

Thank you for the strength given by your incitement.

Thank you for your guidance and your watchful eye on my progress.

Thank you for the changes that make the space for healing and growth,

And gaining of my own self-sovereignty.

Honor to you, An Mórrígan.

Go raibh maith agat.

153.

Hear my prayer, An Mórrígan.

Honor to you, sovereignty Goddess of Ireland.

Sovereignty Goddess, you have defended your people by removing false kings.

You grant and remove the sovereignty of rulers, as needed,

For the good of the people and the land.

I give honor and respect to your judgment, Great Queen,

Guardian of the land and guardian of rightful rulership.

May the unworthy and corrupt rulers fall,

And may better rulers rise in power to replace them.

May the land and its people find their peace and abundance

With the benefits of right-rulership

And the justice and wisdom from worthy leadership.

Thank you, Great Queen, for the changes you are bringing.

My devotion to you, An Mórrígan, the unconquerable Great Queen.

My loyalty to you always.

Go raibh maith agat.

154.

An Mórrígan, hear my prayer.

Receive my offerings, Great Queen.

May my efforts be aligned to the healing and knowledge I seek.

See my efforts to study and learn about you in the lore.

May I see you, as I learn about you, and work with you.

Goddess of Sovereignty, you have helped me regain my self, my honest truth,

And helped me develop and establish self-sovereignty.

May I never lose myself again.

I know you expect much, as you deserve much.

I know that my work for you will be constant.

May I have the resources I need to finish the tasks you have given me.

May I be self-sufficient and maintain my self-care,

So I can maintain my strength on this journey.

This path is a long one, but may I follow it till its completion.

I honor you always, An Mórrígan.

Go raibh maith agat.

155.

An Mórrígan, hear my prayer.

I give my deepest respect to you at all times and I thank you for your time.

shape-shifting Goddess, your form changed by your will,

By your strategy, and by your power.

Sorceress, magic was wielded by you to weaken the enemies of your people.

Prophecies and incitements are given by you, Great Queen,

Goddess whose pleasure is in mustered hosts.

You lead your followers and defend them.

You bring them to the battles they need to face.

Your give incitement to aid them in their battles,

And to finish the work you give to them.

Great Queen, giver of prophecy, battle, sovereignty, and guardianship,

You bring the changes that support justice and bring the battles for needed change.

May your changes bring justice, rightness, and sustained peace.

You are the Great Queen. I honor you.

Go raibh maith agat.

156.

I call to you, An Mórrígan, Goddess most powerful and fierce.

You are welcome here, seer of both victory and defeat on the battlefield.

Goddess that spoke prophecies of a time of abundance and peace

And prophecies foretelling a time of ruin and doom, I honor you.

Shape-shifting Goddess, who can be all things as she desires,

Springs of craftiness and sources of bitter fighting,

An Mórrígan, I honor you.

May I follow your leading, Goddess,

For you bring the needed change and the necessary battles for my growth.

May I find the place of courage and strength that lies within me.

May I never see my battles as a burden, Great Queen,

But may I see them as the source of wisdom and growth that they are.

May there become a wealth of peace within me.

May I find my anchor in these times of change.

May your incitement bring me victory in my battles.

Mighty Goddess, powerful and fierce, hear me.

An Mórrígan, I honor you now and I will continue to honor you always.

My deepest respect to you.

Go raibh maith agat.

157.

An Mórrígan, Goddess that brings forth the greatness from within the broken,

And reveals the strength and sovereignty within,

Hear this prayer that I offer to you.

Honor to you, Great Queen. I honor you forever.

Goddess that brings the gift of facing personal battles,

Working with and embracing the shadow, integrating the shadow-self,

And the healing and growth that comes from that.

An Mórrígan, Goddess that guides to the achievement of self-sovereignty

And to a path walked with rightness and honor, I honor you.

May your changes within me provide the way for triumph and growth.

I will set my hand to the work I have committed to you with renewed vigor.

May I approach the situations in my life with wisdom. May my security be assured.

May I act with honor. May I seek rightness.

Go raibh maith agat. I honor you, Great Queen.

158.

An Mórrígan, Goddess of sovereignty, hear my prayer.

I honor you, Goddess that brings victory to those you gather near to you

By showing them their own strength.

You strengthen your follows and empower them to face their battles,

And you bring them the battles they must face.

I honor you, Goddess that brings what is needed for growth

And what is needed to achieve self-sovereignty.

I honor you, Goddess that brings justice.

I honor you, Goddess that brings change.

An Mórrígan, with trust I embrace what is needed for my growth,

And I commit to the work you have given me.

Thank you for showing me my capability of facing my own battles

And for helping me see my worthiness to face them.

I honor you, Great Queen.

Go raibh maith agat.

159.

An Mórrígan, hear my prayer.

I honor you, the Great Queen and ancient goddess,

Giver of prophecy, strategist with great purpose,

Weaver of incitement through the giving of battle-poetry,

You lead your followers to the necessary battles that bring change.

Honor to you, Goddess of sovereignty,

Battle-crow that speaks prophecies of both victory and doom.

May there be doom to leaders that have lost their honor,

May the corrupt lose their power,

And may the oppressive lose their reign.

Honor to you, An Mórrígan.

Honor to you, shape-shifting Goddess that takes many forms.

Honor to you, Goddess that brings the challenges

That lead to healing and growth.

Go raibh maith agat.

### Prayer of Invocation for Making an Formal Contract

This prayer is an example of a format that could be used to make a contract with the Mórrígan. Again, I am not an expert on the Mórrígan. My opinions on making contracts with her is based primarily on my personal experiences, there has been some reflection (in a limited amount) of shared experiences of others, but I can only speak from my own experience. I'm sharing my personal beliefs with the hope that they may be a helpful viewpoint to consider (not to influence). This information and any guidance I have provided is based on my UPG (unverified personal gnosis). I did feel specifically led to include this section of prayers that could be used - whether whole or in part - when creating a contract with the Mórrígan. I have written these prayers, as I felt led, to the best of my ability.

I feel it's important to say that I don't believe that it's necessary to do ritual or even lengthy prayers to create a contract with the Mórrígan. When I entered into a contract with her I said a simple heartfelt prayer, gave an offering, and wrote it down in my journal after saying my chosen words to her. That's it. I had spoken with her about it beforehand and I received a sense that what I proposed was accepted. Afterwards, I received a sign that was absolutely unmistakable to me and I felt her presence very strongly.

I have received (and to continue to receive, as it was a lifetime agreement) every single thing I have asked for. Trust me when I say that I will do everything in my power to be faithful to my agreement, as if my life depended on it. I have no regrets. Everything I have experienced has been to my benefit and for the most part, my experiences have been positive (as long as I'm doing the work).

The most important thing is to be as specific as possible and to follow through with whatever you are exchanging. I personally don't believe it is necessary to have a contract to work with An Mórrígan or that contracts need to be long-term. It is a very personal and potentially life-altering choice to make an agreement with a God. If you do decide that you want to create a contract, you want to be as specific as possible. Tell her your needs and what you're offering her in exchange. If you wish, it can be as open-ended as to answer whenever called upon and do whatever work is asked of you for a certain length of time (leaving the manner and the intensity of the work to be determined by her), or it can be as specific as creating one piece of devotional artwork each month in exchange for her guidance with finding and maintaining gainful employment. It's also my belief that no matter what you promise, you will also be required to maintain your relationship with her in a method that is appropriate and respectful - this often includes offerings/devotions, study, and prayer. Please alter this prayer to fit your needs. Add or remove whatever feels right.

When planning your contract, make sure to be as specific as possible, proceed with caution, be aware of possible loopholes, only agree to give what is yours to give, and only agree to what you feel you can accomplish. I also strongly recommend adding timelines and asking for your mundane needs to be met easily so that you can focus on the work. I recommend having an established relationship with her first and to consider a contract that is for a limited amount of time. Once a contract is made, stick to what you've agreed to no matter what happens. Whatever you commit to is on you. If you cannot keep your agreement, change your mind, or if you want out after formalizing a contract with An Mórrígan, be prepared for fallout.

Both the work and the rewards are significant. In my personal experience, she is aware of what I am capable of. As long as my efforts are sincere and consistent (allowing for self-care), and I push myself as I am able, she has been satisfied with that. She has let me know what she wants from me as we have worked together. I feel it's important to say that the amount of work has increased as my ability to do my work has increased. I have also been given space to recover in the times that I've needed it, when I asked for it.

Making a contract with An Mórrígan is a very personal choice and should be taken seriously. I am not saying there is anything to fear, but I am also not saying there is nothing to fear. I take no responsibility for any commitments made to the Mórrígan. This is your choice and I cannot dissuade or persuade you. I am sharing information from my personal experiences as directed from her. If assistance is needed, I recommend reaching out to an established pagan priest that is dedicated to An Mórrígan.

As you make your commitment, I recommend giving an offering. Fresh water alone is fine. From what I have read, she is partial to whiskey. In my experience, fruit and dairy are received well. Please be careful and responsible with fire safety if you light a candle. Listen to your intuition and provide what you are able to. The prayer is broken into sections, so you can insert your clearly stated offer where it feels best to you.

Before committing to a contract, I would ask that you take the time to watch these two YouTube videos created by Lora O'Brien. There is truly no one I trust more when it comes to guidance on the Mórrígan and I believe that these videos contain important information that should be strongly considered first. The first video is, "Working with the Mórrígan - Irish Celtic Gods and Goddesses" https://youtu.be/ymlqL7m0OyQ (O'Brien, 2018,YouTube). The second video is, "Mórrígan Q&A Day 1 - Contracts and Agreements" https://youtu.be/Dw8GcmY1zOU (O'Brien, 2019, YouTube). Thank you.

As for my myself, I have had several short-term contracts I've completed with An Mórrígan and I have an overarching lifetime contract with her as well. This collection of prayers was written in due to a (shorter time-frame) contract. It is an offering, promised to the great Queen and I received something specific for it. It had to be completed within a certain time-frame with certain requirements. I know of people that renew their contract annually on Samhain and others that work with the Mórrígan with no contract at all. Contracts do not need to be intentionally difficult or have a myriad of promises, but whatever is agreed to must be completed. I imagine that, if needed, there may be a possibility of renegotiation. While I have never explored that personally, I believe that depending on the terms of renegotiation and if she agrees to it (which she may not), then it may be a possibility. It may not need being said, but choose what you commit to wisely, and follow through.

Consider all possibilities first, and if you believe that a contract is appropriate for you and your relationship with the Mórrígan, I hope that this prayer (or any portion of it) may serve you well if you chose to use any portion of it.

160.

An Mór Ríoghain,

Giver of battle poetry and prophecy,

Inciter of the battle,

Bringer of change,

Present on the battlefield

Sacred sovereignty,

fistfuls of blood,

Prophecies, sorcery, shape-shifting

Satirist, wielder of magic,

Pleasure in mustered hosts,

Incitement of the warrior, strategist,

Guardian of the land,

Bestowing of rulership,

Demanding of sovereignty,

Washer at the ford,

Giving prophecy of doom,

Death to kings with broken geasa,

Restorer of right rulership,

Sovereignty eternal,

An Mórrígan, you are very welcome here.

An Mórrígan, hear my voice.

Goddess, I call out to you respectfully with an offer of contract,

To offer my service to you in formal agreement,

May it be a sacred binding between us, Goddess.

Hear my call and consider my offer, An Mórrígan, Great Queen.

See me. Hear me. Know me. I am here, Goddess.

An Mórrígan, I understand the seriousness of an agreement with you

And I offer my commitment to you with respect.

Within the time-frame agreed upon, when you call for me,

I will be present for you and fulfill my obligations.

An Mórrígan, I know it is expected of me to always keep my word

And to never leave a promise to you unfulfilled.

I will be responsible for what I promise to you.

I will be accountable for the work you expect from me.

I will be honest with you always and loyal to you.

I understand that once my offer is accepted by you,

It is permanent unless you tell me otherwise.

Mighty and powerful, An Mórrígan, I honor you

And I am grateful for the relationship between us.

Hear my voice and this offer I make to you.

My desire is to honor you in the ways I can be useful to you, An Mórrígan,

And to do work that is worthy.

May I be respectful of your boundaries

And appropriate in my manner towards you.

I honor you, Great Queen. I will be faithful to any agreement between us.

I will never betray you even if you choose to release me from your service.

I will be loyal to you always, An Mórrígan.

Thank you for hearing my offer of a contract with you.

Send me a sign, Goddess, if you accept it. I will be faithful to our agreement.

I offer you my fealty and this offer of an agreement to you in a formal contract.

I will put my sincerest effort into the work that you give to me.

May I know, with a sign that is unmistakable to me, if you accept it.

May nothing deter me from any agreement we enter into together.

I offer this to you with my deepest respect, An Mórrígan.

Honor to you, Great Queen. Go raibh maith agat.

## Prayers of Gratitude

161.

Honor to you, An Mórrígan. Praise to you, Great Queen.

Hear my prayer, this offering of words.

I have come to give you my gratitude, sacred and generous Goddess.

Thank you for your aid in the times that I have most needed it.

Thank you for keeping me in safety, as I do my work,

And as I live my life, Great Queen.

Thank you for your guidance and insight.

Thank you for your support and protection.

Thank you for evolving me, through the lessons you give me,

Into a stronger version of myself.

Thank you for the opportunities you have sent to me.

I honor you, An Mórrígan. You are the Great Queen,

The powerful shape-shifting Goddess,

The mighty satirist, that none would dare cross.

May I always give you the honor you deserve.

Honor to you and your plans for change in this world.

You will always have my loyalty.

May my service and my commitment honor you, Goddess.

I thank you for this opportunity to work together.

Thank you, Great Queen, for your support I have received while we work together.

Honor you forever, An Mórrígan! Praise to you, Great Queen! Go raibh maith agat.

162.

An Mórrígan, hear my voice as I offer this prayer of gratitude to you.

Thank you, Goddess, for contributing so greatly to my life

And helping me find my way to my healing, self-worth, and sovereignty.

Thank you for your guidance with my work to integrate my shadow-self

And when facing my challenges and conflicts.

Thank you for staying with me in times of struggle and for keeping me from harm.

May I be of use to you, An Mórrígan. May my efforts honor you, Goddess.

May I see the opportunities to support positive changes within myself

And to support the work of others, when requested and appropriate.

May I live honorably. May I not disappoint you.

Honor to you, Goddess that has guided me to the path that leads to self-sovereignty.

I thank you, An Mórrígan, for your guidance, your protection, and your support.

I will faithfully give you my loyalty and devotion, Great Queen.

Go raibh maith agat.

163.

An Mórrígan, hear this prayer and receive my offerings.

I honor you, Great Queen.

Thank you for your guidance as I work towards my goals.

Thank you for this work that you've brought to me.

Thank you, Goddess, for the relationship we've built

And that we're continuing to build together.

Great Queen, I honor you and I will faithfully keep to my promises to you.

I will attend to my work and my self-care, may I have your guidance with both.

May I hear and understand your guidance when it comes.

I will stay true to this path. Watch over me, Great Queen, as I walk it.

Honor to you forever, An Mórrígan. Praise and honor to you, Mórrígu.

May I complete my work with rightness and resolve, in your name, as directed.

You have my fealty, my service, and my loyalty, An Mórrígan.

I offer you space within me, if you wish for that,

In the times that you deem it appropriate or necessary.

May I give you the time and space in my life that is needed,

To do the work you require of me. Thank you for the work we do together.

Thank you for hearing my voice and this prayer, An Mórrígan.

Praise and honor to you, Great Queen.

Go raibh maith agat.

164.

Hear my prayer, An Mórrígan, and receive my offerings.

Goddess that shows the ways to recover self-sovereignty, I honor you.

An Mórrígan, Sovereignty Goddess of Ireland, thank you for guiding me

To rediscover that I have power within myself

And for inspiring me to rise up and take control of my life and my choices.

Thank you for showing me that no one is coming to save me,

That I have the power within to save myself

And that no one else needs to be my savior,

And to push back against my doubts and fears surrounding that.

Thank you for giving me your guidance and direction

And for keeping me in safety while I find my footing in my life.

May I be steadfast with my shadow work and turn my love inwards.

May invest in my own overall well-being and health

As I work towards inner healing and wholeness.

May my actions and choices be aligned with the plans you have for me,

And the work you have chosen for me to do.

Thank you, Great Queen.

Go raibh maith agat.

165.

An Mórrígan, hear my prayer.

I honor you, Great Queen, eternal and sovereign Goddess.

Thank you for watching my progress and guiding me in it.

Thank you for helping understand the changes I need

And the mindsets I need to release.

Thank you for helping me free myself from the indoctrination that no longer benefits me,

And for the guidance that has set me on the path I'm on now,

A path that has led me to myself.

Thank you for the work you've brought me, An Mórrígan.

In the ways I can support your plans for change, may I be present and capable.

With your guidance, Great Queen, may I clearly understand

And keep my focus on the work you bring me.

I honor you, Great Queen, and I will honor all of our agreements.

May I be resolute and successful in the work you give me.

May I bring the best of myself to your service.

May my efforts honor you, An Mórrígan. May I be useful to you.

I am here for you with the best of what I have to offer.

Go raibh maith agat.

166.

Honor to you, An Mórrígan, shape-shifting Goddess

That invokes courage and strength before the battle through incitement.

Goddess that brings the transformations that lead to self-sovereignty

Through the facing of inner battles and bringing about necessary changes,

An Mórrígan, I honor you. Thank you for working with me as I grow more capable.

Thank you for the growth I've experienced and the changes that happened in my life.

Thank you for the work you have brought to me, Great Queen,

And the opportunities I have received to contribute. May my efforts be worthy of you.

May safety stay with me, as I do the work I have committed to you.

May I complete my work with devotion and resolve, in your name, An Mórrígan.

May it honor you. I am here, Goddess, and I will answer when you call for me.

Thank you for hearing my prayers and for the time you've invested in me.

Go raibh maith agat

167.

An Mórrigan, hear my prayer. Great Queen, I honor you.

Giver of battle-poetry and prophecy,

I give you my gratitude for the many ways you have helped me.

May I remain willing to accept changes that need to take place in my life.

Thank you, Goddess, for putting me on the path to self-sovereignty

And for the tasks you give me, both now and in the future.

May I not disappoint you, Great Queen, with your guidance

May I correct my course as needed.

May my behavior and my intent be aligned with rightness.

An Mórrigan, I honor you now and I will honor you always.

Go raibh maith agat.

168.

An Mórrígan, Goddess of sovereignty and battle, hear my prayer.

Goddess, I call out to you with my gratitude.

Thank you for helping me have security with my mundane needs,

So I can focus on my work I've committed to you.

Thank you for your guidance, Goddess,

Especially on the work needed for my spiritual growth.

Whatever battles I need to face within myself, may I face them with courage.

May I unlearn any unworthy principles that I have been indoctrinated into

Whether or not I am aware of them.

May I have a clear understanding on how to act with rightness,

And understand what rightness means to me in my life.

Great Queen, may I find my footing and my strength,

As I put forth my efforts to the work I have been given.

May I be responsible for the completion of my tasks

And remain accountable to myself and to you, Great Queen.

I honor you, An Mórrígan, Goddess that I am devoted to.

Go raibh maith agat.

169.

Hear my prayer, Mórrígu. I will honor you always, Great Queen.

I give you my deepest respect and my gratitude, Goddess.

I embrace this path you have led me to and I thank you

For the sense of purpose I have found with the work you bring me

And the growth that it has caused in me.

Thank you for the time you've given me, Goddess, as I've found my way.

Thank you for your guidance as I continue with the work needed for my healing and well-being.

May I have the wisdom to be honest with myself as I move forward in my life

And continue to consider the truths that have emerged from my shadow work.

May I work for you in any way that you have need of me

And may I find triumph in my battles for self-sovereignty.

I am devoted to you, An Mórrígan, and will be faithful to the work you have given me.

I will continue on this path, with all I can sincerely give,

And be faithful to the promises I have made to you, Great Queen.

With your guidance, may I support my momentum by investing in well-being and self-care.

Thank you for your time and for hearing me, Great Queen.

An Mórrígan, I honor you now and I will honor you always.

Go raibh maith agat.

170.

Hear my prayer, An Mórrígan, and receive my offerings.

I honor you, Irish Goddess concerned with sovereignty, right rulership,

And sacred guardianship of the land.

I give you my devotion, An Mórrígan, thank you for working with me.

May I do the work needed to remove any harmful conditioning from my behavior,

And be emboldened to reclaim all parts of myself and defend my self-sovereignty.

I will not give away my power. I will not deny myself the gift of accountability.

May I have the courage to stand for my own truth whenever necessary.

Thank you, Great Queen, for the changes I've experienced with your guidance.

Thank you for your aid and for your support, Goddess.

I will remain faithful as I walk on this path of study, service, and training,

As I continue to build our relationship that we have together.

An Mórrígan, you are worthy of all my efforts

And I give them to you with my deepest respect.

I will remain faithful to the work you give me as we work together

Throughout the whole of my life, if you desire it.

Thank you for the path you have brought me on.

I will remain loyal to it and I will remain loyal to you.

I honor you, An Mórrígan. I thank you, Great Queen.

Go raibh maith agat.

## Prayers of Dedication to the An Mórrígan

171.

Hear my voice, An Mórrígan, Goddess of sovereignty and battle.

I honor you and I welcome you, Great Queen.

I call out to you with a promise to give you my continued devotion.

An Mórrígan, I dedicate myself to the work we will do together.

I commit myself to move forward on this path with you.

I give you my word, you have devotion and my promise,

I will do the work you give me to the best of my ability.

I will continue to support my growth and beneficial changes in my life.

Hear my prayer and my promise, Great Queen.

Go raibh maith agat.

172.

An Mórrígan, Goddess of battle and sovereignty,

Goddess over warriors and warriorship, hear my prayer.

Great Queen. I call to you to give you my promise.

I promise you my willingness to do the work you give me, as I am able,

And to act honorably in my life.

Hear this oath, An Mórrígan. I have thoroughly contemplated my promise

And the weight of this commitment. I promise you my effort and devotion.

Powerful An Mórrígan, Goddess that brings in victory in battle,

With your guidance, I will face my battles and support your work with my efforts.

I will work for you and with you, as you will have me, Great Queen.

An Mórrígan, I promise you my undying loyalty and devotion.

I will study, bring you offerings and prayers, and will do acts of service as I am able.

I'll listen for your guidance. May I hear you clearly, An Mórrígan.

I honor you always, Great Queen.

Go raibh maith agat.

173.

Praise and honor to you, An Mórrígan, hear my prayer. I honor you, Great Queen.

I am grateful about the relationship that we have built together,

For the work that we have done together,

For the work the work that I continue to do in your name,

And for the guidance you have given me in my life, Great Queen.

Great Queen, I offer you formal commitment to work together,

A long term working relationship with my continued devotion to you.

An Mórrígan, Goddess of sovereignty, battle, prophesy, and incitement,

Prophetess, sorceress, red-haired satirist, bringer of change, giver of victory, I honor you.

An Mórrígan, I dedicate myself to you with my promise of loyalty and commitment.

May I honor you with the work I do and by living my life honorably.

May I honor you by the offerings and devotions I bring to your altar daily.

I will do the work you bring me to the best of my ability, Great Queen.

Hear this sacred promise that I give to you, Goddess. I will be faithful to it.

Honor to you always, An Mórrígan.

Go raibh maith agat.

174.

An Mórrígan, hear my prayer. An Mórrígan, I call to you. I invite you.

Honor to you mighty goddess, with my respect and fierce love,

I honor you Great Queen. Hear my prayer. See me. Know me.

With devotion, with eyes wide open, I dedicate myself to your service, An Mórrígan.

I commit to investing in my own healing, my training, growth, and self care.

May I be prepared to work, to embrace the good work never-ending for a right purpose.

May I not be afraid of the changes that are coming.

May I put in the effort to dismantle any colonial mindsets within me.

May I be prepared to maintain the needs of my mundane life.

May I set aside space daily for offerings, attention, and time with you.

I honor you, An Mórrígan, Goddess of battle and sovereignty.

May I never neglect any promise made to you.

My loyalty to you always. Guide me as we work together.

I am in your service Great Queen.

May my dedication be received by you.

Go raibh maith agat.

## Prayers to Macha

175.

Macha, hear my prayer. I honor you.

Goddess, whose masts were the heads of slaughtered men,

I ask for your help to find justice in my life.

Goddess that met injustice with vengeance

And delivered a curse that was unbreakable

To nine generations of the men of Ulster,

Hear my prayer and see the injustice done to me.

I ask for your aid, Macha.

I ask for an intervention of justice to unfold in my life.

May justice be dealt against those that have harmed me

And those precious to me.

Blessed Macha, sovereignty Goddess, defender of women and children,

Deliverer of justice, I honor you.

May I receive fair treatment and a return of security.

Hear me, Macha, giver of justice. I honor you, Goddess.

Go raibh maith agat.

176.

Praise and honor to you, Macha. Giver and deliverer of justice, defender of women

And protector of women in childbirth and labor, I honor you.

Hear this prayer I offer to you, Goddess.

Macha, wife of Crunniuc, woman from the fairy hill,

You ran against the king's horses and won.

You delivered justice against those that made you race before dying in childbirth.

The curse you gave matched the humiliation and cruelty

Done to you and it lasted for nine generations.

Macha, I honor you.

Macha Mong-Ruadh, you claimed the throne that was yours by right,

And when you were denied, due to being a woman, you took it by battle.

You kept your throne by sovereignty, rightness, honor, and battle.

You delivered justice against those that denied you your throne,

That tried to take your throne from you, and that tried to assault you.

You are the only queen named among the high kings of Ireland.

Queen Macha, I honor you.

Macha Daughter of Ernmas, sister of the Mórrígan and Badb,

Sorceresses of the Tuatha De Danann, battle Goddesses, and women of power,

You fought for and alongside your people against the Fir Bolg.

You worked sorcery with your sisters and cast magic against the enemies of your people.

In the battle against the Fomorians, you fought for your people

And died on the battlefield alongside Nuada, the first king.

Macha, I honor you.

Macha, wife of Nemed, you died clearing plains for farming.

And as a seer, you foresaw much, and foresaw the Táin Bó Cúailnge.

Macha, I honor you.

Macha, daughter of Partholon, you were among the first people in Ireland.

Macha I honor you.

Macha, giver and deliverer of justice, defender of women and children,

Protector of women in childbirth and labor, Goddess of justice,

I honor you, Goddess, giver of justice. Praise and honor to you, Macha.

Go raibh maith agat.

177.

Honor to you Macha, defender of women and children.

Honor to you Macha, Goddess that intervenes in the causes of injustice.

Macha, deliverer of justice, I honor you.

Thank you for your time and for hearing my prayer, Goddess.

May I be led to the ways I can effectively support

The causes for justice in this world.

May I have the courage to stand and hold space for justice

In the times I witness injustice in my life.

May I examine myself for any behaviors or mindsets

That contribute to injustice, and may I correct any I find.

May I live a life of rightness and honor in every way I am able.

May I have the strength to stand for the causes of justice

And to hold space for justice. I honor you, Macha.

Go raibh maith agat.

## Prayers to Badb

178.

Honor and praise to you, Badb.

Hear this prayer spoken to honor you, Goddess.

Washer at the ford, giver of prophecy,

Sacred Goddess, I honor you.

You are the remover of false kings,

Of kings that have broken their geasa and lost their honor,

Removal of fallen kings, all so that rightful kings can rise

For the good of the people and the survival of the tribe.

Honor to you, Badb, washer at the ford.

Battle crow above the battlefield, observant of the battle

And aiding your favored side.

Battle crow on the battlefield,

Present on the battlefield. Bringing horror to the enemy.

Washer at the ford, giver of prophecy,

Battle crow, queen of war, I honor you.

Goddess that leads to the shadow-self within

For the strength, wisdom, and healing therein.

May I integrate my shadow, for the strength, wisdom,

And healing that it will bring.

Honor to you, Babd.

Go raibh maith agat.

179.

An Badb, hear my prayer. I honor you.

Goddess that speaks prophecies and sees all,

I ask that you help me to see and understand the information

Provided to me through divination. May I see all truths given to me with clarity

And may I be aware of any way my projections alter the information.

May I have the wisdom to ask specifically for the insight I need

And not be distracted by questions that do not benefit me.

May I intuitively understand the answers that already exist within me.

May I be given insight into messages given to me

Through divination I use

And insights into omens and dreams given to me.

I also ask for guidance when I reach into my sacred darkness within,

When I do my shadow work, and when I reach into my traumas

To see healing, wisdom, and growth.

May I receive the gift of foresight, through your guidance, great Babd.

May I gain the wisdom I need to thrive successfully in my life,

Clear and beneficial guidance regarding all things necessary for my work,

And the wisdom to apply that knowledge to my choices I make.

Honor and praise to you, Badb, Washer at the ford, Giver of Prophecy,

Harbinger of doom to kings that have broken their geasa. I honor you, Goddess.

Go raibh maith agat.

180.

Red-mouthed Badb, washer at the ford and queen of war, I honor you.

Hear my prayer, ancient and powerful Goddess.

Daughter of Ernmas, sorceress and prophetess may I be guided by you

As I do my shadow work. Hooded crow that influences battle,

May I be aided with my shadow work

And never fear as I reach deeply into my darkness within.

May I be blessed with wisdom, Badb, as I face what lies in my depths.

May my journey honor you, great Badb.

Watch over my journey through death, when that time comes.

Honor to you, Badb. I call to you with great respect. Hear me, Goddess.

Praise and honor to you, great Goddess.

Go raibh maith agat.

## Prayers to Nemain

181.

Hear my prayer, Nemain, and may it honor you.

I call to you with great respect.

Nemain, queen of war and wife of Neit,

Ancient and sacred Goddess,

Frenzy of battle, bathed in blood,

Goddess above the battle encampment,

Above the swords, spears, and shields,

Shrieking and causing confusion below,

Praise and honor to you, Goddess.

Law giver, sacred venom, giver of triumph and terror,

I ask for your aid with respect and devotion.

May there be no rest for those that sincerely wish me harm,

Or knowingly interfere with the progress on my path,

While my efforts are to live a life of victory and rightness.

Nemain, may you bring confusion and horror to my enemies with your shrieking.

May I be kept from harm, Goddess.

I honor you, unfathomable and unconquerable Nemain.

Honor to you forever, Goddess, frenzy of battle bathed in blood.

Honor to you bringer of terror and confusion to the enemy.

Honor and praise to you, sacred queen of war.

Go raibh maith agat.

182.

Honor to you, Nemain. I call to you with my deepest respect.

Queen of war and wife of Neit. Sacred and ancient Goddess that invokes the frenzy of battle

And brings confusion to the encampment of the enemy, I honor you.

Generous Nemain, I ask for your aid and offer you my devotion.

If I have enemies, may confusion be brought upon them

And may they no longer have the capacity to plan any action against me.

May my enemies be scattered. May my enemies have no power against me,

And may their their words be useless against me.

May the intentions of my enemies, if their intention is against me,

Crumble beneath them and become nothing but dust upon the earth.

May my enemies stay far away from me and take no action against me

So that I can have peace in my life

And do the work that is worthy in safety and without distraction.

Hear me Nemain, I call to you with a need that is honest and sincere,

And I ask only for the safety of all that is precious to me.

Goddess of battle, warfare, and the frenzy of war,

I ask for your shrieking to be put on my enemies acting against me,

So that I can have peace to do my work for Na Mórrígna.

I will continue to honor you with my prayers and offerings.

I will always speak your name with honor, sacred Goddess.

Nemain, I honor you and I will be faithful to my promise of devotion.

Honor to you, great and powerful Goddess. Go raibh maith agat.

183.

Honor to you Nemain. I call to you with admiration, respect, and devotion.

Nemain, well-acquainted with the blood of the battlefield,

Goddess that invokes frenzy in warriors engaged in battle, I honor you.

Law giver and sacred venom,

Many died of terror on the night you shrieked above the battle encampment.

Nemain, queen of war, frenzy of battle, fury and terror, I honor you.

I ask for your aid, Goddess that invokes terror. Set your sight on my enemies,

So that safety and security is returned to me.

I ask that any plots against me, known or unknown,

Fail without harm done to me or those belonging to me.

Hear my prayer, Nemain, I ask for your aid with the deepest respect,

And as a devotee of Na Mórrígna. You have my gratitude, always.

May I be safeguarded, sacred and ancient Goddess.

My need is sincere and my devotion is faithful.

I honor you, Nemain.

Go raibh maith agat.

## Prayer to Fea

184.

Praise and honor to you Fea,

Sacred divine mystery and queen of war.

Wife of Neit, daughter of Elcmar, sister of Nemain,

Goddess shrouded in secret and the unknown, hear my prayer.

Honor to you Fea, I come to you with respect and devotion.

I ask for your guidance as I seek the shadowy parts of myself that I do not understand.

May I find a way to communicate what isn't easily expressed from within myself.

May I have access to the most obscure parts of myself, in order to gain wisdom, healing, and peace.

I honor you, Fea. I give honor to Na Mórrígna.

In the naming of the land, Fea's Plain, Mag Fea was named for you, and is yours.

Goddess that inspires the wisdom of the unknown within, I honor you.

Honor to you, Fea. Thank you for your time and your aid, mighty Goddess.

Thank you for your guidance.

Go raibh maith agat.

# Prayer to Bé Neit

185.

Honor to you, Bé Neit, sacred queen of war.

Woman of war, you give triumph to champions and warriors engaged in battle,

Granting victory to your favored side and aiding in the battle

By giving terror to the enemy.

I honor you, Bé Neit, wife of Neit, Goddess that brings victory in battle.

I call out to you, Goddess, with great respect.

May I have victory and triumph in my battles,

And may I stand victorious in the face of my challenges.

May I remember that I am worthy of my battles

And that my battles belong to me.

I honor you, Bé Neit, with loyalty to you and all Na Mórrígna.

Honor you, Goddess of battle, Goddess of war, Goddess of fury and strength in battle.

Honor to you sacred Goddess.

Go raibh maith agat.

## Prayer to Anu

186.

Praise and honor to you, Anu. Goddess, hear my prayer.

Greatness wealth, greatness of abundance, and beauty of the fertile land.

Feminine shape and curve of the land,

In the naming of the land, the Paps of Anu were named for you and are yours.

Goddess connected to the land, through the abundance of the land you provide security

And support the well-being of your people.

Goddess, I ask that wealth and abundance stay with me

So that my security and well-being is supported and maintained.

Thank you, Goddess, for your blessing and your support.

I honor you, Anu. I will say your name with respect

And offer you prayers in my devotion. Honor to you, Anu.

Treasure of the land, prosperity of the land, wealth of the land,

Fertility of the land, abundance of the land, and beauty of the land, I honor you.

Anu, treasure of the land, prosperity of the land, wealth of the land,

Fertility of the land, abundance of the land, beauty of the land, I honor you.

Honor to Na Mórrígna, forever.

Go raibh maith agat.

## Personal Prayers

187.

May it honor you, Great Queen, when I have accountability for myself,

And with every choice I make that is more honorable.

May it honor you when I consider the rightness of my actions

And examine what needs to be changed in my life and my mindsets.

May it honor you in the times I support and hold support space for justice,

In whatever ways I am able,

When before you, I wouldn't have.

May it honor you, An Mórrígan, when I see the injustice in the world

And when I stop to listen when others tell their stories,

When before you, I wouldn't have.

May it honor you when I see the truth rather than trying to run from it

And when I take action as far as my reach will allow.

May I honor you, Great Queen, when I have the courage to believe

That my future isn't dictated by my past,

When I pull away from distractions and see the world around me,

And when I take back my power over myself to become self-governing.

May it honor you, An Mórrígan, when reclaim my self-sovereignty,

Embrace accountability, and live a life that is resoundingly my own

In the ways that are sacred to me.

May it honor you, Great Queen, when I live honestly and fiercely,

And when I yearn to learn more.

May it honor you, Great Queen, that I have gratitude for you.

No matter what I may have lost, I have gained back myself.

May I honor you, An Mórrígan, as long as I live my life.

Great Queen, as I learn to truly respect myself and others,

And to connect to the earth and community,

May I learn how to heal and grow to become a better person.

However I choose to live my life as it evolves and changes,

I will honor you and be faithful to you, An Mórrígan.

My loyalty to you, forever.

Go raibh maith agat.

188.

Gratitude to you, An Mórrígan,

Great Queen, hear my voice and my prayer.

I offer you words of praise and respect,

Offerings of service and fealty,

My devotion and dedication with faithful love and respect.

I give my hope for continued relationship,

My hope of my continued growth and success,

And my promise to always keep my word to you, Goddess.

An Mórrígan, Great Queen, I honor you.

Powerful Sorceress, Shapeshifter Goddess,

Renowned satirist, I honor you always.

Hear my call, An Mórrígan. I give you my gratitude, Great Queen.

An Mórrígan, mighty Goddess of sovereignty and battle,

May I be strongly rooted as an oak tree to the land.

On my path, may I be strong and immovable,

Against the challenges and battles I may face.

May I stand strong and not be torn down by any storm.

May I be full of crops on my branches,

Good fruit on my branches for harvest, in my time,

And nourished by the land and the waters below me

May I be nourished by the sun and the air above me.

May I be safe and strong throughout the journey of my life.

I give my gratitude to you, An Mórrígan.

I honor you this day, Great Queen, and I will honor you all of my days,

For the remainder of this lifetime. May I be long-lived and serve you well, Mórrígu.

Hear this prayer and receive my offerings.

Praise to you, unconquerable Great Queen.

Go raibh maith agat.

189.

Honor to you, An Mórrígan, Irish sovereignty Goddess.

Thank you for your guidance when I struggle to find direction.

Goddess that requires growth and change,

Thank you for bringing to my attention to the changes needed in my life,

And for bringing about the changes needed

When I have struggled to let go.

Thank you, generous Goddess, for your time and your patience with me,

As I've worked to find my footing and am finally beginning to learn.

Thank you for working with me, as I unlearn so much that has built up over time.

Thank you, An Mórrígan, wielder of magic and sovereignty unyielding.

Thank you for the shadow work you've triggered,

When I've needed the push to embrace it.

I am grateful to see the realities of my past and the dishonor in many of my actions,

To witness my traumas rather than hiding from them,

And to be aware of the abuse done to me and the abuses done by me in my past.

I am grateful for the knowledge of it all, and with that truth, to be empowered to make choices.

May I actively work to become the better version of myself,

Living a life as closely aligned with rightness as I can,

And with healing and regaining of my own sovereignty.

May I not be ashamed of myself.

An Mórrígan, with your guidance, may I learn how to become the unfailing shield

To defend my self sovereignty and the value of my authentic self.

As I defend my own sovereignty, Great Queen, may I support the sovereignty of others.

May I hold space for the voices being denied the space to speak,

And listen to the truths of others.

May I learn to do the work needed to have a sense of community and hospitality.

May I see the opportunities to contribute positively

Within the communities I am a part of,

And may I have skills, resources, and abilities to contribute successfully.

May I sincerely invest my effort in the work you've given me

And may I do my work honorably.

May I stand unafraid of what the future will place on my path

And of what battles I may one day face.

May I work through my battles and see my truth.

May I gain my sovereignty over myself and defend it.

May I take back control of my own life,

And live a better life because of it.

May I be awakened to my battle. May I rise and take hold.

I call out to you with my greatest respect, Great Queen.

I thank you for hearing them, Goddess.

You have my loyalty and my devotion, always, An Mórrígan.

Honor to you forever, Great Queen. Go raibh maith agat.

190.

An Mórrígan, Shapeshifiting Goddess,

You have taken the shape of beasts that occupy land, sea, and sky,

As wolf, heifer, eel, and crow.

Red-haired Satirist with red eyebrows,

Your name was given as, "keen edged, small lipped,

Plain cloaked, hair, sharp shouting fierceness, a phantom."

An Mórrígan, I call out to you with respect to honor you.

Goddess, I thank you for challenging me to become a better version of myself,

For guiding me in the ways to become more capable of the work you give me,

And for giving me the work that has helped me to achieve growth

And strength in my life. Thank you, Great Queen. You have my devotion.

You have my gratitude forever, An Mórrígan.

My respect and loyalty to you always, Great Queen.

Go raibh maith agat.

191.

Praise and honor to you An Mórrígan,

Shape-shifting Goddess, red haired satirist,

Bringer of cattle raids, sovereignty, sorcery, and poetry.

An Mórrígan, Goddess that brings the battles necessary for change, I honor you.

Goddess that brings work to her followers, to aid her great work, I honor you.

Goddess that has brought me to face my battles for sovereignty and change,

Thank you for helping me recover my sense of dignity within

And the fight to care about who I am and what I have.

May I continue my work to gain self sovereignty

And reclaim all of myself.

May I have peace with the knowledge that my internal work

Will continue throughout all of my life.

Uncover the bones of the buried traumas with me, Goddess. May I face them all.

An Mór Ríoghain, may I pull down the walls of I've hidden behind,

May your crows tear them down with me. May I see the truth

And burn away any lies that have festered within.

May I discover the reasons why I listened to them and fed them.

May the trauma beneath my scars be remembered fully

And may I have the strength and resolve to work through them.

May I honor you, Great Queen, with the internal work I do.

May I take on, with honor, the great work that lies before me.

I will face it and embrace the full reality of my life thus far.

I will heal and not deny myself the gifts of truth and accountability.

I will not deny myself the task of my own healing,

And I will work through my grief and remorse.

I will see it through to the other side.

May I embrace the generous and merciful parts of my character

And give love to myself within.

Freedom waits for me. My healing waits.

May I unlearn what I need to and may I learn what I need to in my life.

May I go onward in that cycle of unlearning, healing, and learning,

And then may I cycle deeper to begin the process again.

I am sick of my internalized fear, and while it is a process,

I am glad to be making progress, no matter how small.

Thank you, Goddess, for guiding me in the ways to break it.

An Mórrígan, may I honor you by doing the work you give me

And making efforts in my life that are sincere and constant.

May I praise you with the acts of devotion I have promised to you.

May I come to your altar with respect.

May I walk this path with the willingness to work and learn.

My devotion, loyalty, and love to you always, An Mórrígan.

I honor you forever, Great Queen.

Go raibh maith agat.

192.

Hear my prayer, An Mórrígan. I honor you, Great Queen.

Thank you for hearing me every time I've come to you, Goddess.

May my actions prove worthy of your guidance

And the time you've invested in my development.

May I prove to be useful to you, Great Queen,

And may I be faithful to all my promises that I have made to you

Throughout this lifetime and may my promises I've made for my next lifetime

Be fulfilled faithfully as well.

I honor you, An Mórrígan, bringer of change.

Through your guidance, may I be brought closer, one step at a time,

Further on this path you have brought me to, Great Queen.

I know this path leads to a place of wisdom, strength, and self sovereignty.

With my acts of devotion given to you, if I miss one day,

May I get back on track the next.

May I learn to limit the distractions in my life, as I am able,

And  keep my mind and my priorities focused on my work.

May I stay encouraged on days that are challenging,

And remember to give myself time and patience as I learn and grow.

May I act honorably and keep my word.

May I live a life aligned with rightness, to the best of my ability,

And continue to do the work I need to, both to honor my commitments,

And to support my own growth.

Thank you, Great Queen, for this opportunity to work together

And for the benefits I have received through this journey.

Great Queen, Goddess of battle and sovereignty,

Thank you for guiding me as I work to achieve victory in the battles I face

And healing from the traumas of my past. Thank you for prompting me

In my shadow work and bringing change to my life.

Thank you for the spiritual experiences I have had and the connection

I feel in our relationship together, An Mórrígan.

I honor you forever, Great Queen.

Goddess of sovereignty and battle, you have my loyalty and devotion.

I am here, Goddess. I will not leave my promises to you unfulfilled.

Praise and honor to you, An Mórrígan.

Go raibh maith agat.

193.

An Mórrígan, hear my prayer. I honor you, Great Queen.

May my efforts to do the work your give me prove to be worthy of you,

And may I respect that the work will not end.

May I appreciate the work and have the strength to embrace it,

Even in the times when it is challenging.

May I find joy in the work, as I am able,

And peace in that fact that it will be ongoing throughout my life.

When the work doesn't end, our relationship continues, Great Queen.

May I honor the work and may my contributions be useful to you.

May my work be never-ending throughout this lifetime and into the next.

I am here, An Mórrígan. I will keep giving whatever efforts I am able,

For as long as able, until I cease drawing breath in this lifetime.

An Mórrígan, sovereignty Goddess of Ireland,

Thank you for the work we do together and the relationship we have built.

May I be useful to you, Great Queen, throughout my life.

Honor to you always, An Mórrígan.

Go raibh maith agat.

194.

The Great Queen that incites the battle to bring changes within,

Hear my prayer and see me in this moment.

I invite the changes needed to become a better human and more effective devotee.

May I be a help to myself and not hinder the growth I am capable of.

May I bring benefit to you and be useful in whatever ways I am able.

May I contribute positively to the communities I am a part of.

May I live my life honorably and hear your guidance when you give it.

May I listen and be aware. May I be open to the experiences you bring me.

Great and powerful Goddess, guide me as I do the work to dismantle

Harmful ideologies and oppressive indoctrination in my life.

Great Queen, may I find the support and resources I need while I do my work.

May I receive the support that will aid me in my efforts

And may I give aid to others as I am able.

May I hear your prompts, Great Queen, when you want me to give my aid.

Thank you, An Mórrígan. I am faithfully devoted to you

And I will give my effort to whatever work you choose to task me with.

I am in your service, Great Queen. I honor you always, An Mórrígan.

Go raibh maith agat.

195.

An Mórrígan, hear my prayer. I honor you, Great Queen.

May my heart keep hope for a better world,

One where leaders have accountability and lead with rightness

And one where corrupt leaders face true justice.

May I stay hopeful for a world where the oppression of people has ended,

And the land, sea, and sky is cared for and defended.

May I believe in a world where people can live with accountability and peace.

May I believe that one day leaders will hold justice as sacred

And care for the needs of their people and the lands they are responsible for

With rightness and honor.

Great Queen, may I not become jaded when I see the injustice in this world,

And may I find the ways I can support positive changes in the communities

I live in and in the communities beyond.

Goddess of sovereignty that brings the needed battles that lead to great change,

I honor you. An Mórrígan, may great changes come to this world,

And may your great work demonstrate the power of change

That leads to sovereignty and rightness.

May the oppressive powers in this world face inescapable justice

For healing of this world and its people.

I honor you, Great Queen. Thank you for hearing my prayer

And receiving my offerings. Praise and honor to you, An Mórrígan.

Go raibh maith agat.

196.

An Mórrígan, battle crow that flies and observes the battle, I honor you.

I have answered your call to face the battles within.

I ask for your support and guidance with the challenging situations I face in life.

Great Queen, you see the bloodied triumphs and the defeats on the battlefield.

You see all that are born in battle. May you see me, Goddess,

When I am born in my own battles.

Guide me, An Mórrígan, to find an anchor of strength and courage within me.

May it honor you when I carry on to face my battles, Great Queen.

When I commit to embracing my personal battle for sovereignty,

And maintain my self care so that I am able to recover while doing my work,

May it honor you, An Mórrígan. Mighty leader and sacred Goddess,

Great Queen, I honor you. Praise and honor to you always.

Go raibh maith agat.

197.

An Mórrígan, Goddess that demands the journey to self-sovereignty,

You have brought me to face myself.

With your guidance, I have been able to recover parts of myself

That were lost, hidden, and buried. I thank you, Goddess.

May I have the solitude and space I need as I work to resolve

The internalized impacts from my trauma.

If there are any rugged and sharp stones within me, blocking my progress,

May I turn over those stones and see what lives on the other side.

May I embrace the most rejected and the abandoned parts of myself,

With my acceptance and love. May I embrace them.

May I see all that exists in my shadow without fear.

I will honor myself with my respect. I will send my love inward. I will choose myself.

May my path become one of rightness and honor.

May I be persistent in my efforts in my devotions. May I stay on the path that honors myself.

I will study. May I listen and learn. May I hear the truth and embrace it.

I will work to refine the skills used to accomplish the work given to me.

I will live my life fully, as I continue to learn and grow stronger on this path, An Mórrígan.

I honor you and I thank you, Great Queen. I am loyal to you and to the work

You have given me. Thank you for supporting me in my growth and healing.

Thank you for your guidance. May I aid you in your great work, An Mórrígan,

In whatever ways I am able. Honor to you forever, Great Queen.

Go raibh maith agat.

198.

Mórrígu, Goddess of sovereignty and battle,

Thank you for leading me to my part in your great work.

May I set my attention on it and may I be passionate and focused.

In your name, An Mórrígan, may I give my efforts and may they be effective.

I will work for you and with you without stopping, An Mórrígan.

May I carry on as honorably as I am able, with rightness and unfailing desire,

To fulfill the promises I have made to you, Goddess.

May my efforts be worthy of you.

Thank you, An Mórrígan, for hearing my prayer.

Guide me as I do the work you bring me in this lifetime.

Shape-shifting Goddess that is unmatched and eternal, I honor you.

I will remain faithful and answer when you call for me, An Mórrígan.

I am loyal to you always. I honor you, Great Queen.

Go raibh maith agat.

199.

An Mórrígan, hear my prayer. I honor you, Mórrígu.

May my offerings be worthy of you and my devotion be unending.

I ask, An Mórrígan, that I have safety and security

For both my household and myself as we work together.

Goddess, may there be no cause to worry about our mundane needs being met,

So that I am able to better focus on the work I have promised to you.

May my household needs be maintained easily and reliably.

May money come to me easily and my financial debts easily leave.

May my employment be easily kept for as long as I desire it.

Goddess, if there is a better place or way to meet my financial needs,

If there is another employer or a different type of work that I should consider,

May I have your guidance, Great Queen.

If there is a change in employment that I should seek out,

To one more aligned with the work I am doing for you,

or that could support your great work in some way,

May I be led in that direction.

May I be willing to embrace changes that will benefit me.

May I have wisdom and necessary caution when making choices

That may impact the security of my household.

May I receive your guidance with the choices I make.

Thank you for your aid, Great Queen, in the times that I have needed it.

An Mórrígan, thank you, for your generosity with me.

May I have the strength and the resources to complete what is asked of me.

May my actions will remain honorable and my devotion remain true.

I honor you, Goddess. My loyalty to you will always be present.

I am in your service and that commitment will follow this lifetime into the next.

I will be faithful, Great Queen, to all I have promised you.

I honor you, An Mórrígan, this day and for all of my days

That exist for me in this lifetime. May I be long-lived.

As your devotee, may my devotions be worthy of you.

As your dedicant, An Mórrígan, may I receive your guidance.

May I know the ways to honor you, Great Queen.

May my determination be unfaltering

As I work to accomplish my tasks steadily and faithfully.

May I find successes with my sincere efforts

To complete all that has been promised to you.

Honor to you forever,  An Mórrígan.

I will be faithfully devoted to you for the rest of my days, Great Queen.

Go raibh maith agat.

200.

An Mórrígan, Goddess of sovereignty, I honor you.

Goddess that has been so generous to me, I give you my gratitude.

You have called me to wake and rise to my battles,

And I am not a warrior, not fully prepared to meet my battles,

But I will do all I can and continue to do so.

May I grow stronger and rise to meet the challenges you give me.

I'll awake and rise to my battles, as give as much as I am able,

Until my time on this earth is done.

Prepare me Great Queen, and I will give my effort.

Guide me, Great Queen, and I will follow your leadership.

Instill within me the ability to see the direction of your call,

And understand the work you want me to do.

May I have the resources, support, and skills to complete it.

I am here on this path to follow it loyally until its end,

Knowing the amount of work you are known to require

Of those that are in your service. May my efforts be worthy.

Thank you for believing in me, An Mórrígan, before I believed in myself.

Thank you for trusting me with the responsibility of your call.

I honor you, Great Queen, with devotion and with my love.

I will follow your guidance with dedication, An Mórrígan. I am here, Goddess.

I will remain loyal to you always. I honor you, An Mórrígan.

Go raibh maith agat.

## Closing Note of Thanks

To whoever finds this book, thank you for reading. I hope this small book is supportive to you on your own path or has given some food for thought. If this book is available for purchase, I will make it as low cost as I am able. If there are ever any profits received on my end from this book, they will go to a charity based in Ireland. While I may not have a way to show you the evidence of this, please know that I have been given that directive from the Great Queen so you can trust that it will be done. As a devotee of the Mórrígan, it has been my intention to honor her with this devotional project and provide inspiration and support for others on their path if possible.

This book is written as an offering to Herself, the Great Queen. Honor and praise to An Mórrígan. I hope that these prayers may be supportive to you on your spiritual path with the Great Queen, her sisters, or Na Mórrígna as you understand them to be. May this contribution be worthy of the Great Queen.

## Recommended Resources

I personally gained a lot from my studies at the Irish Pagan School with Lora O'Brien, The Book of the Great Queen by Morpheus Ravenna, and the Pagan Portals books The Morrigan: Meeting the Great Queens and Raven Goddess: Going Deeper with the Morrigan both written by Morgan Daimler. There are many other reliable sources that reference the ancient Irish lore. I also strongly recommend Lora O'Brien's YouTube video playlist on the Mórrígan. There is a wealth of invaluable information there on the Mórrígan, and excellent information on Irish paganism throughout all of their content. Finally, I would like to recommend WAR GODDESS: The Morrígan and her Germano-Celtic Counterparts A dissertation by Angelique Gulermovich Epstein.

I have included a few links to resources and for as a reference for some of the lore referenced in a few prayers. Please note, these included links were active at the time of publication.


The link which references the Mórrígan's abode is in the Metrical Dindshenchas, for poem/story 49, is https://celt.ucc.ie//published/T106500D/index.html (the link will take you to the main page and left for poem/story 49 on the left. The link for information on Oweynagat Cave can be found on the website for the Rathcroghan visitor center at https://www.rathcroghan.ie/


The section of Irish lore where An Mórrígan takes the shape of a wolf, eel, and heifer is found in the Táin Bó Cúailnge. The Táin also has the passage where An Mórrígan speaks to the Donn Cuailnge (Brown Bull of Cooley). Online copies of the Táin can be found on several websites, including, http://adminstaff.vassar.edu/sttaylor/Cooley/


The An Mórrígan's name was given as, "keen edged, small lipped, plain cloaked, hair, sharp shouting fierceness, a phantom" in the Táin Bó Regamna. This is also where An Mórrígan was described as being a woman with red hair and red eyebrows. A link to a translation of the Táin Bó

Regamna online is https://lairbhan.blogspot.com/2015/03/tain-bo-regamna.html. The translation is by

Morgan Daimler (2015).


Shared/mentioned content from Lora O'Brien and the IPS:

O'Brien, L., Lora O'Brien at Irish Pagan School, (2008, October 7)

      https://loraobrien.ie/morrigan/

O'Brien, L., Lora O'Brien at Irish Pagan School, (n.d.)

      https://loraobrien.ie/morrigan-irish-mythology/

O'Brien, L. (2019, November 1). Mórrígan Q&A Day 1 - Contracts and Agreements. YouTube.

      Retrieved October 30, 2021, https://youtu.be/Dw8GcmY1zOU

O'Brien, L. (2008, October 7). The Mórrígan - playlist. YouTube. Retrieved October 30, 2021, from

      https://www.youtube.com/playlist?list=PL9QXQd7GCJnravcRxxPmp-lUPReUN9aPp.

O'Brien, L. (2018, November 28). Working with the Mórrígan - Irish Celtic Gods and Goddesses.

      YouTube. Retrieved October 30, 2021, https://youtu.be/ymlqL7m0OyQ


Links for Irish lore:

http://www.maryjones.us/ctexts/index_irish.html

https://www.duchas.ie/en


Links for resources on Irish history:

https://loraobrien.ie/irish-history-books-recommended-resources/

https://rarebooks.library.nd.edu/collections/irish_studies/index.shtml

https://www.museum.ie/en-IE/Collections-Research/Online-Galleries/Online-Galleries

https://www.ucd.ie/irishfolklore/en/

Links for Irish pronunciation:

https://www.teanglann.ie/en/

https://www.focloir.ie/en/dictionary/ei/pronunciation

Honor to the Great Queen!

Praise and honor to An Mórrígan, forever!

Mórrígan Abú!

Printed in Great Britain
by Amazon

16846203R00132